I'm Going To WRITE!™

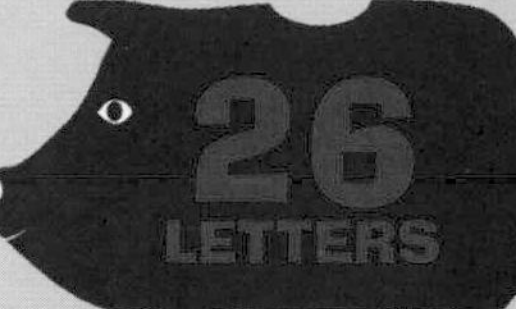

UPPERCASE LETTERS

STERLING CHILDREN'S BOOKS
New York

In this book you will learn how to write these letters and numbers.

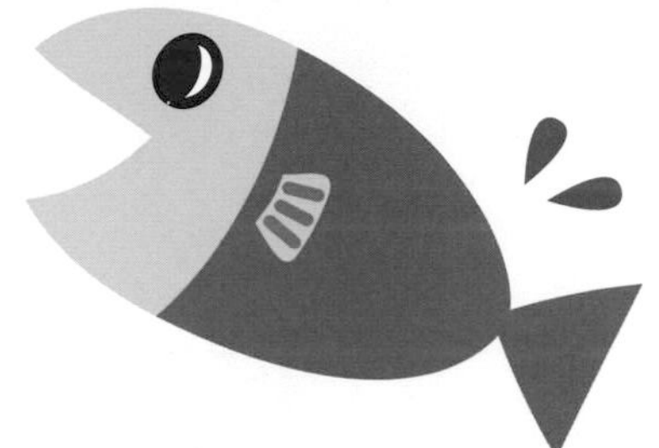

A B C D E F

G H I J K

L M N O P

Q R S T

U V W X Y Z

1 2 3 4 5

6 7 8 9 10

Writing

LION

Trace.

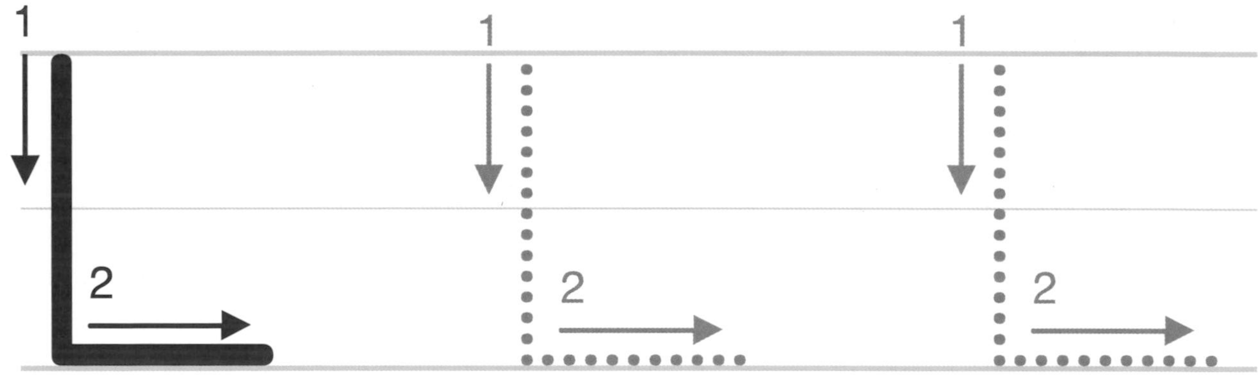

Write on your own.

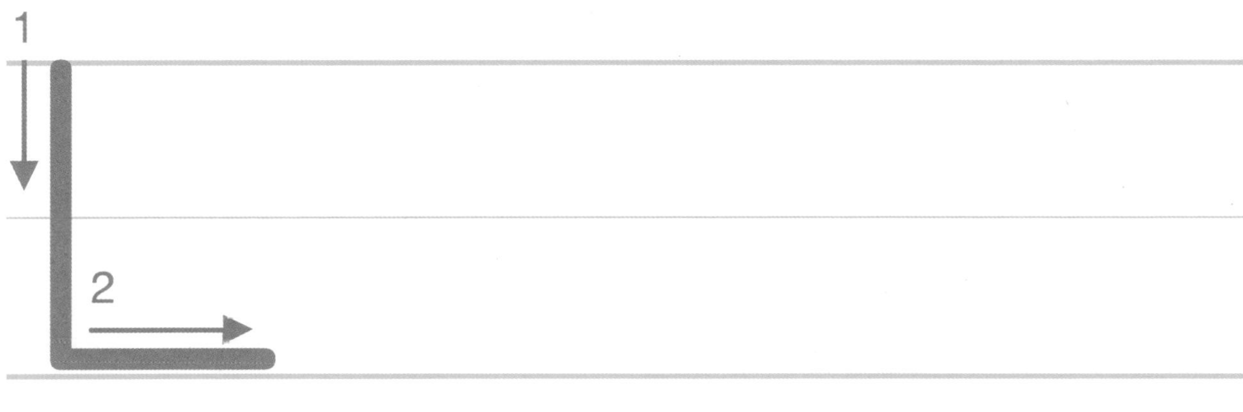

LITTLE

LIGHT

A B C D E F G H I J K L M N O P Q R S **T** U V W X Y Z

Writing

TOYS

Trace.

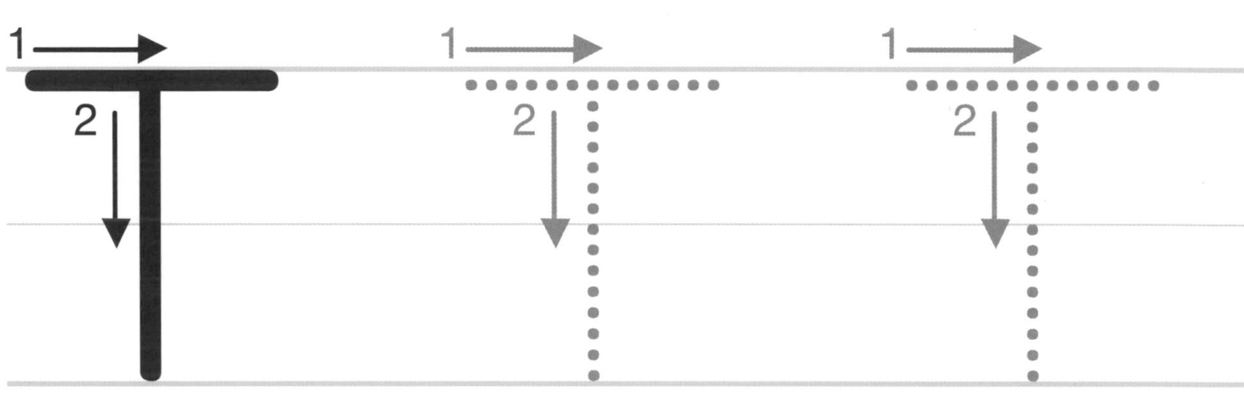

Write on your own.

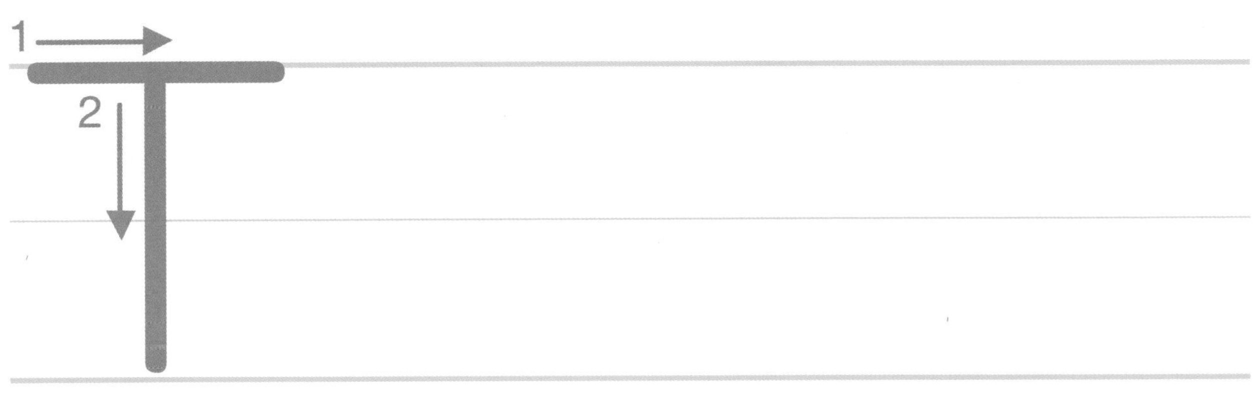

TRAY

TRUCK

Writing

HOUSE

Trace.

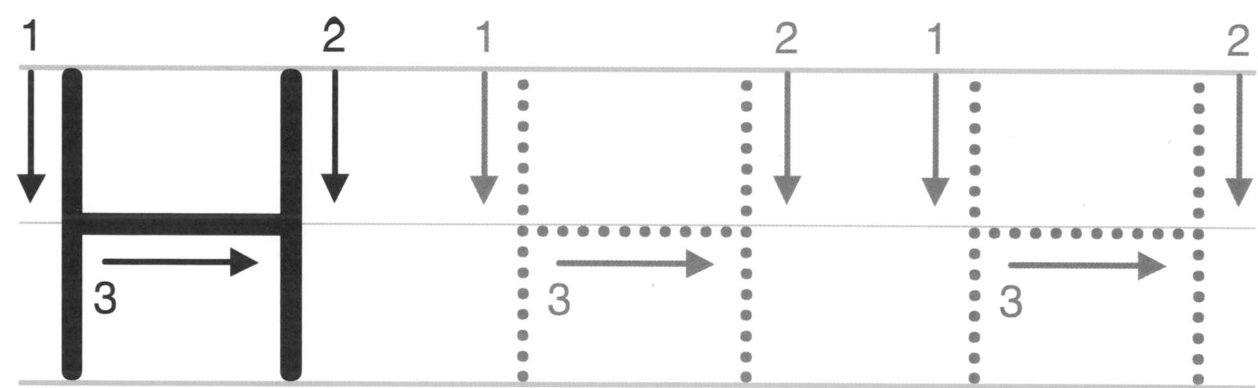

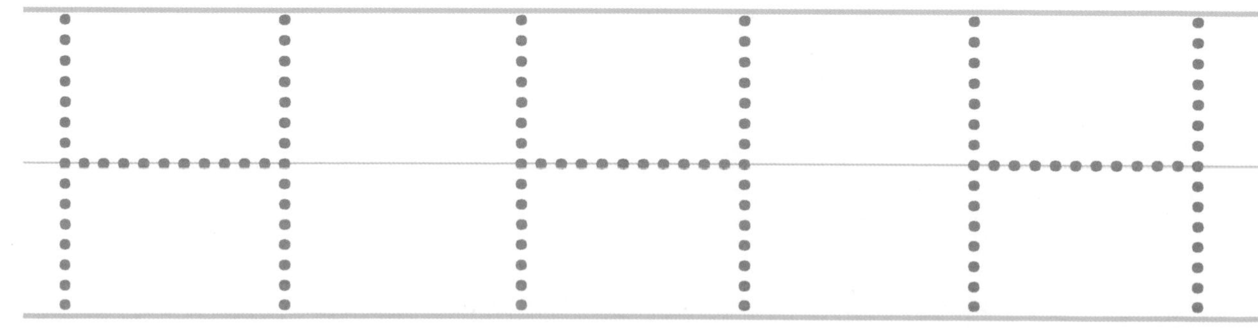

Write on your own.

HAND

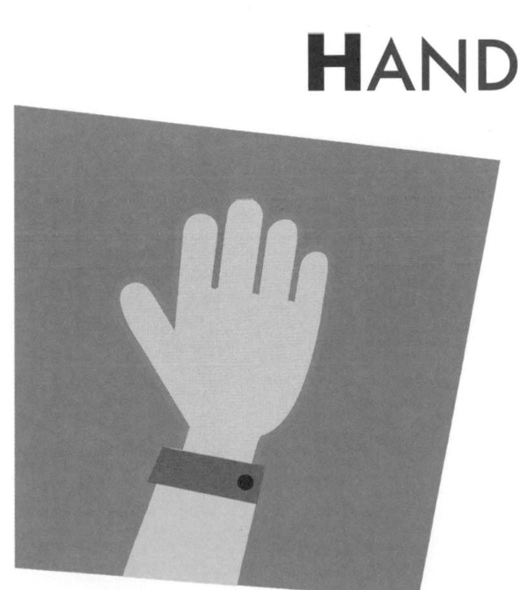

Writing

INSECT

Trace.

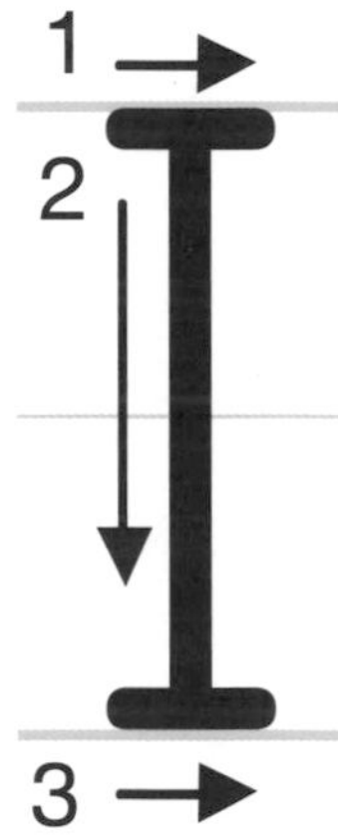

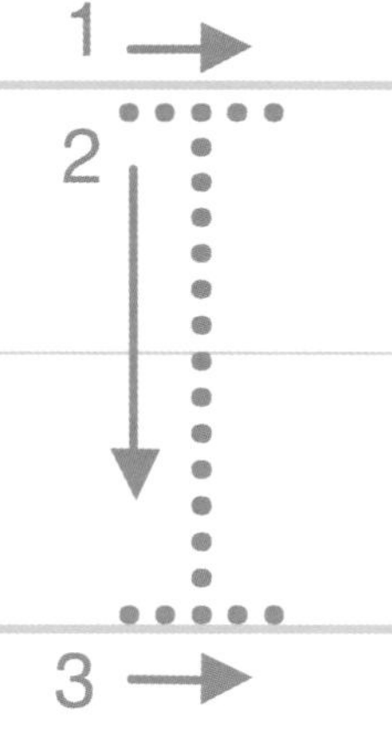

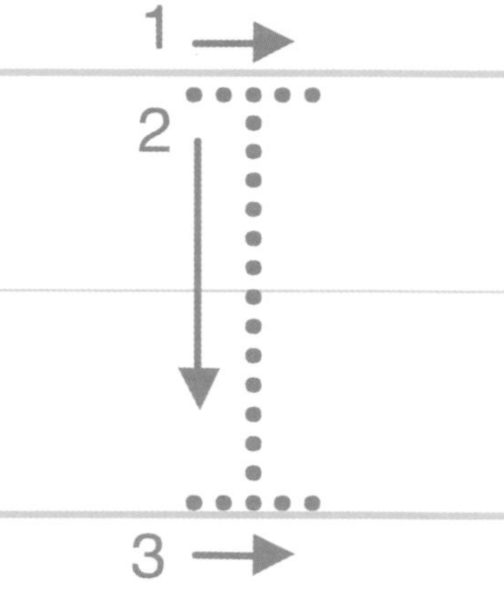

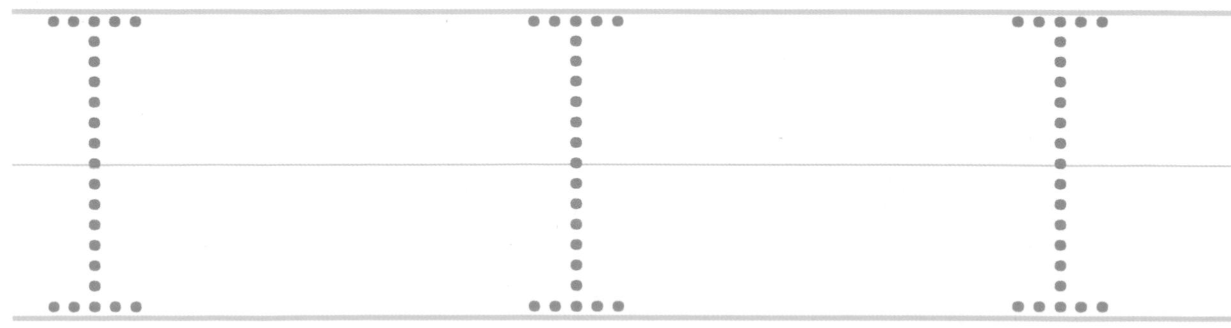

Write on your own.

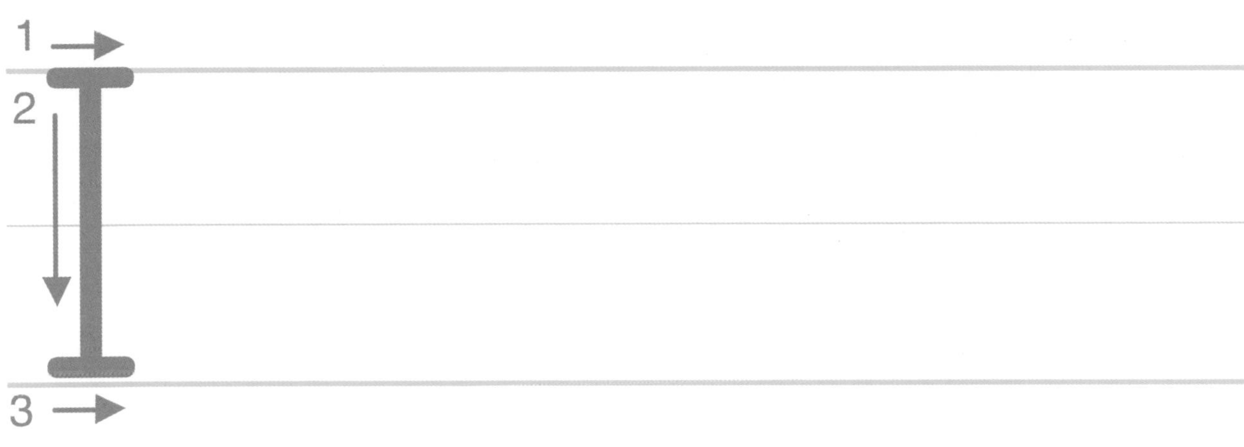

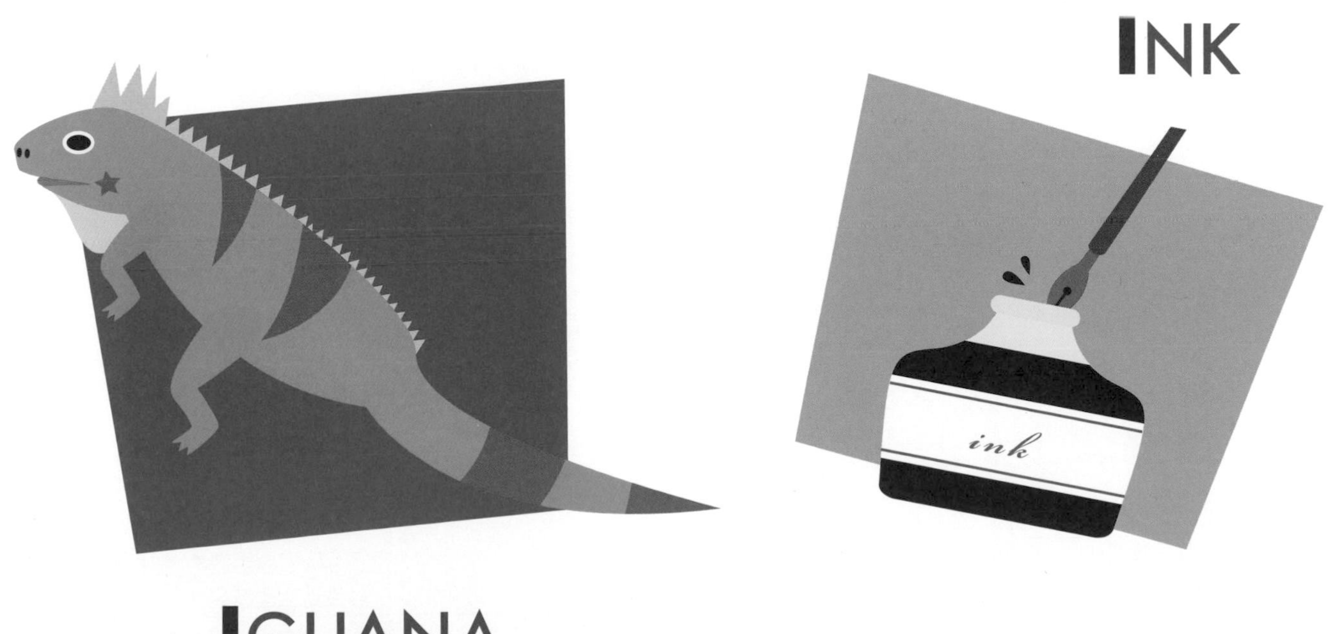

A B C D E F G H I J K L M N O P Q R S T U V W X Y Z

Writing

FRIENDS

Trace.

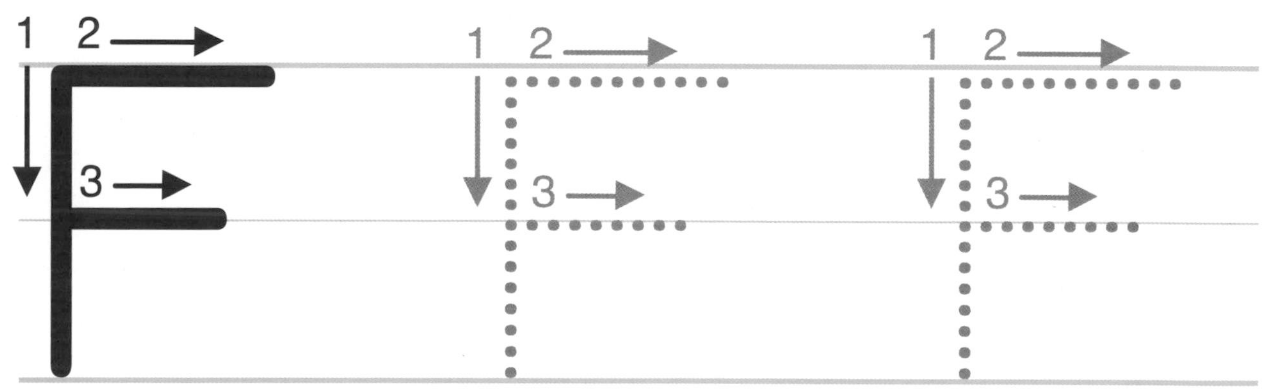

Write on your own.

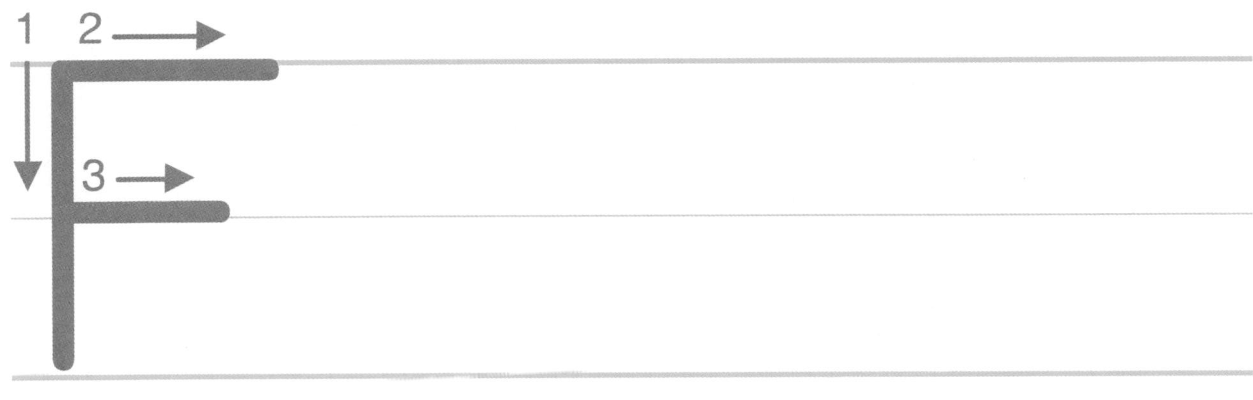

FRIES

FISH

A B C D E F G H I J K L M N O P Q R S T U V W X Y Z

Writing

EAT

Trace.

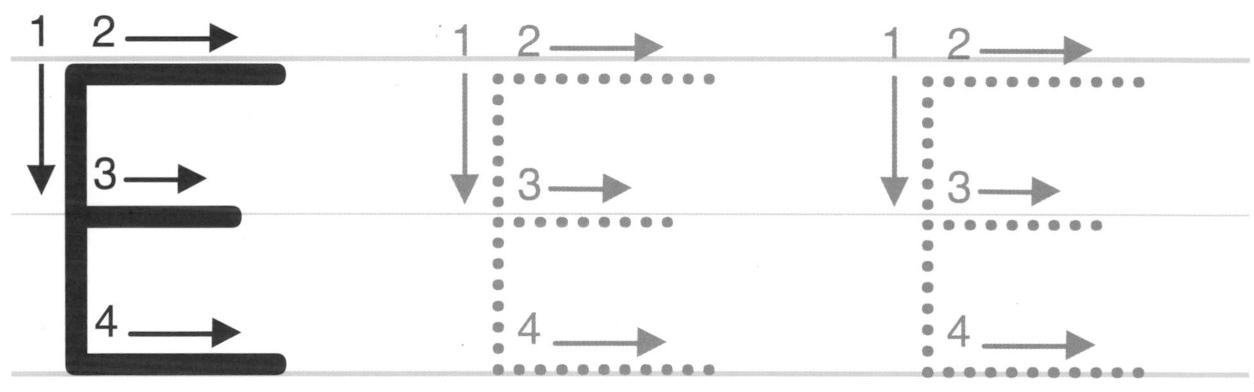

Write on your own.

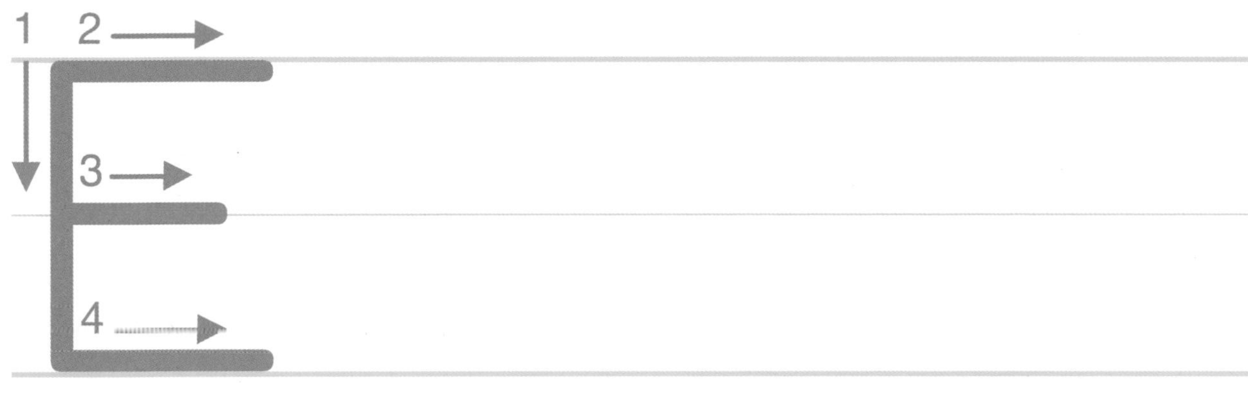

EGG

EMERALD

A B C D E F G H I J K L M N O P Q R S T U V W X Y Z

Writing

XYLOPHONE

Trace.

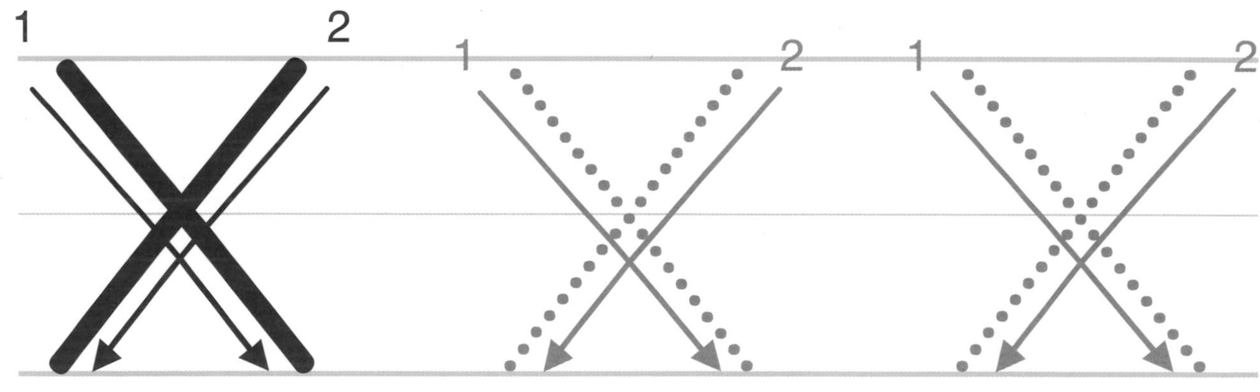

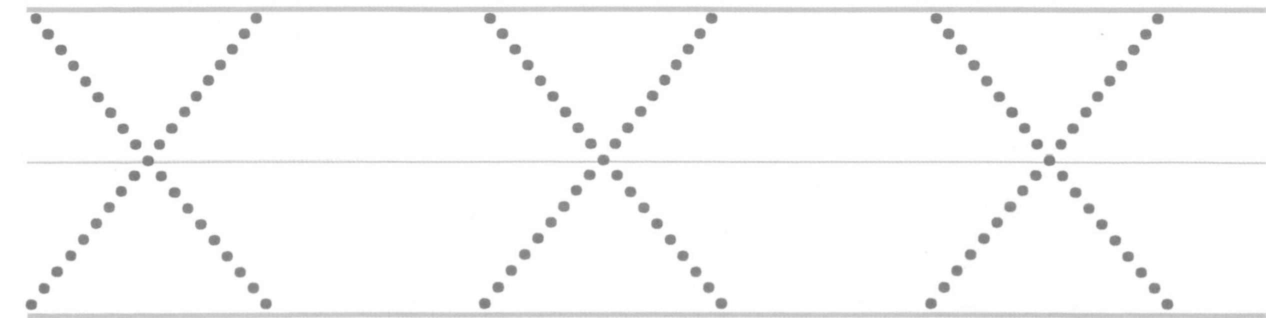

Write on your own.

X-RAY

E**X**IT

Writing

VALENTINE

Trace.

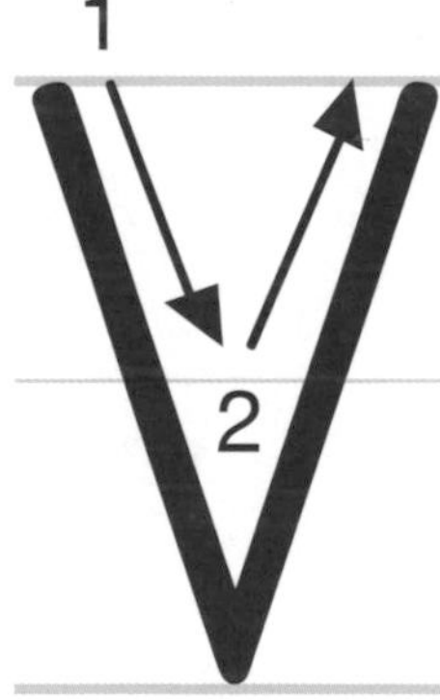

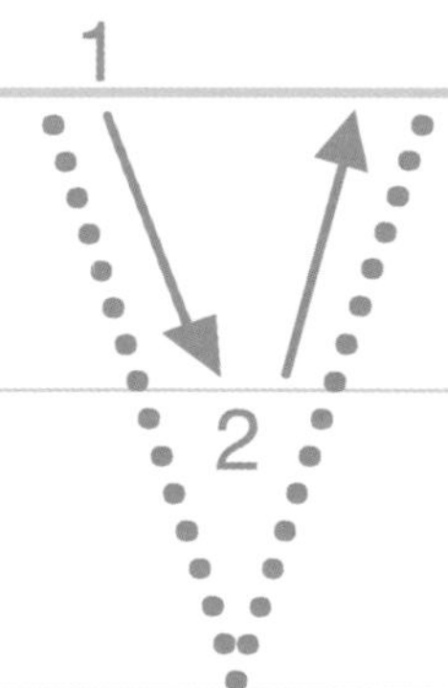

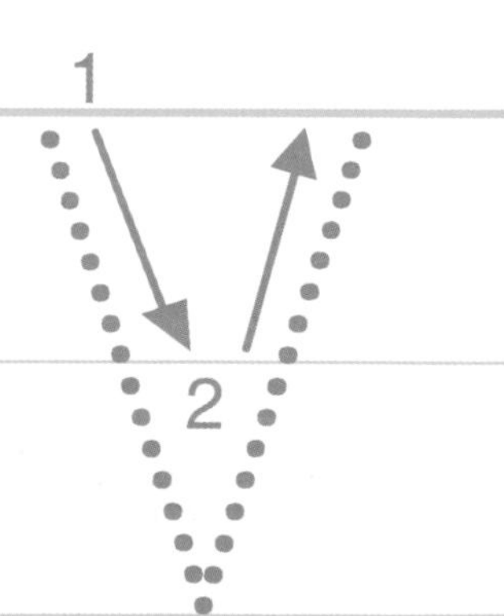

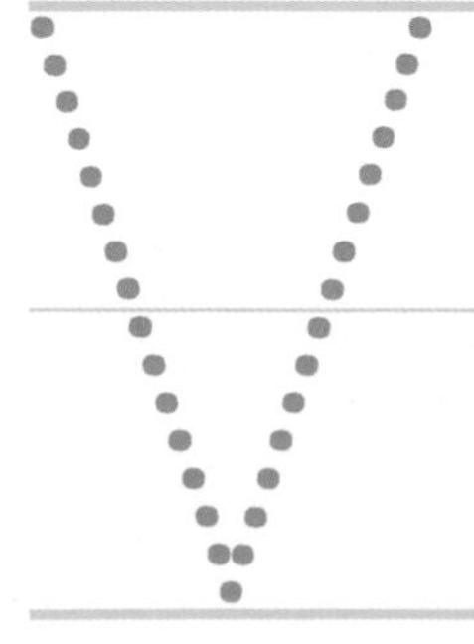

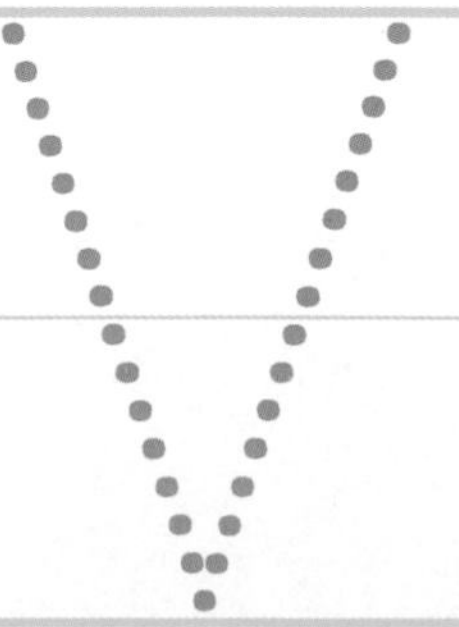

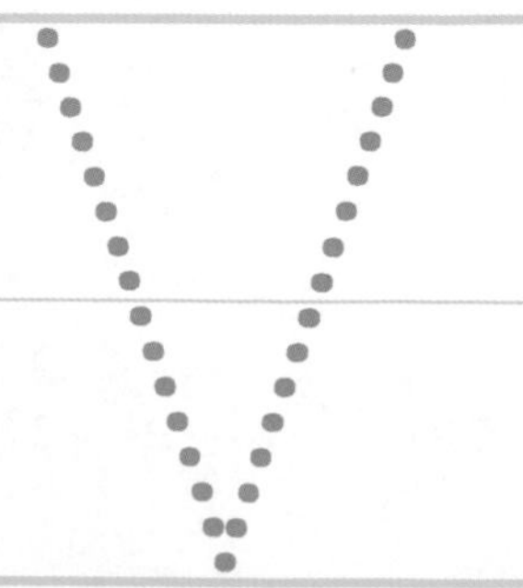

Write on your own.

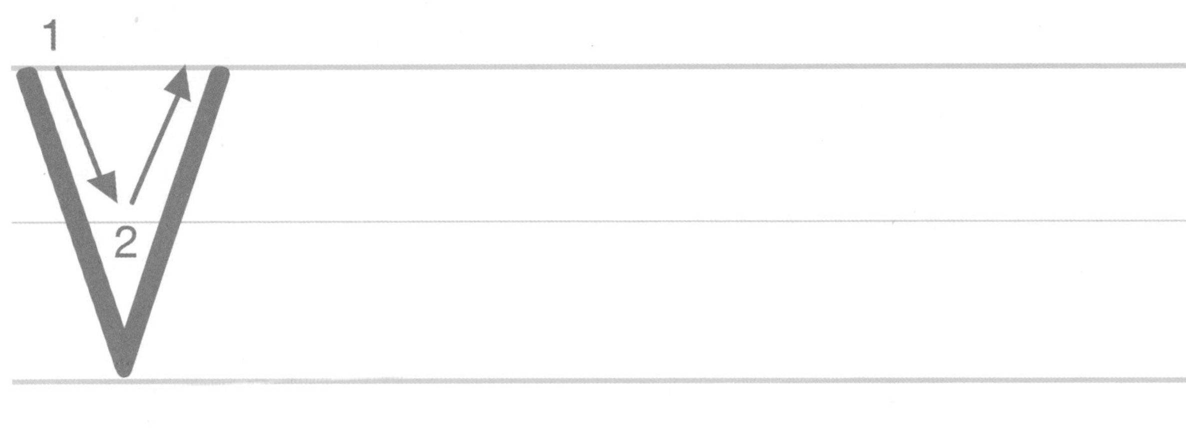

VASE

VAN

Writing

YO-YO

Trace.

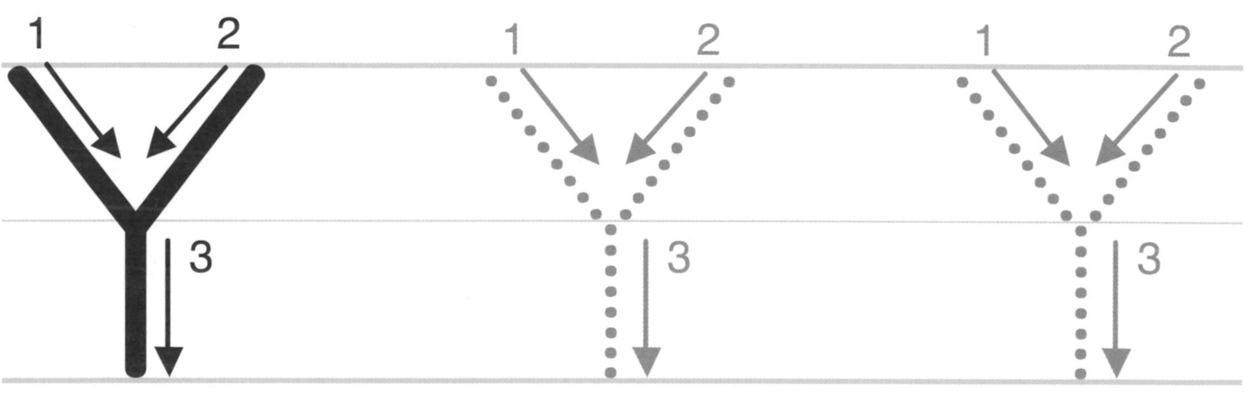

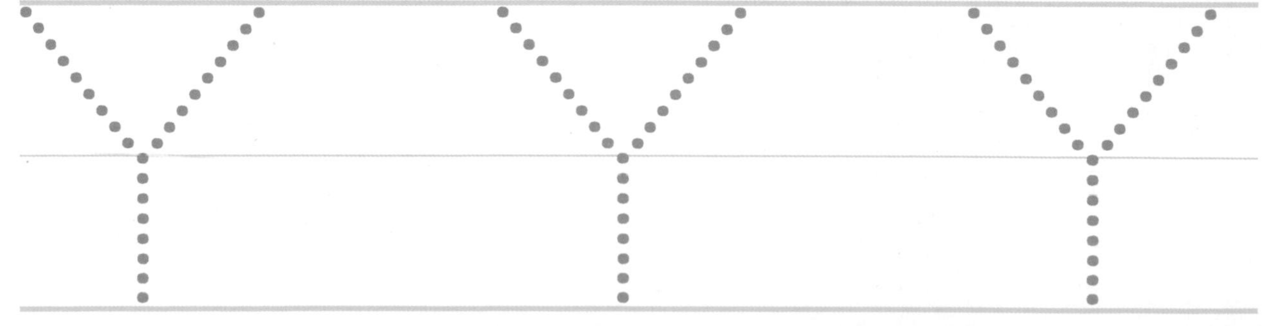

Write on your own.

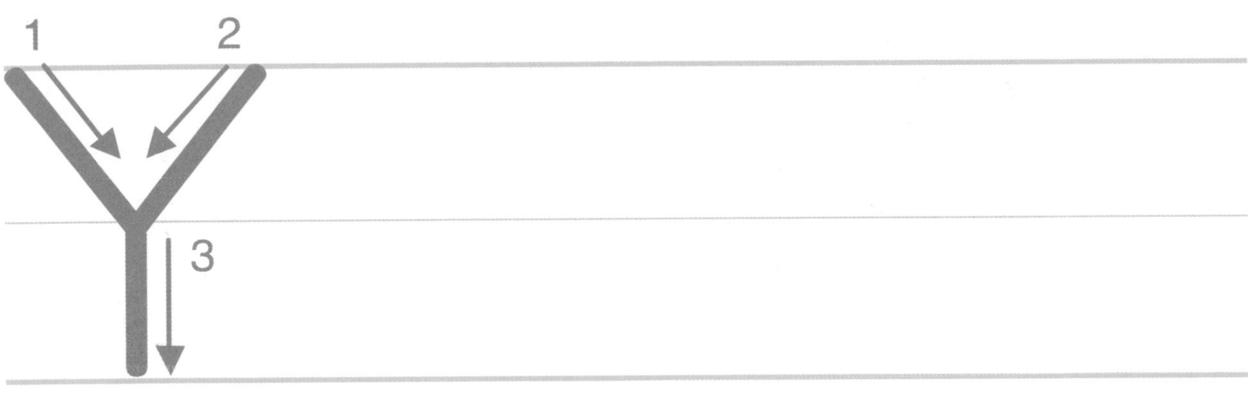

YARN

Writing

NIGHT

Trace.

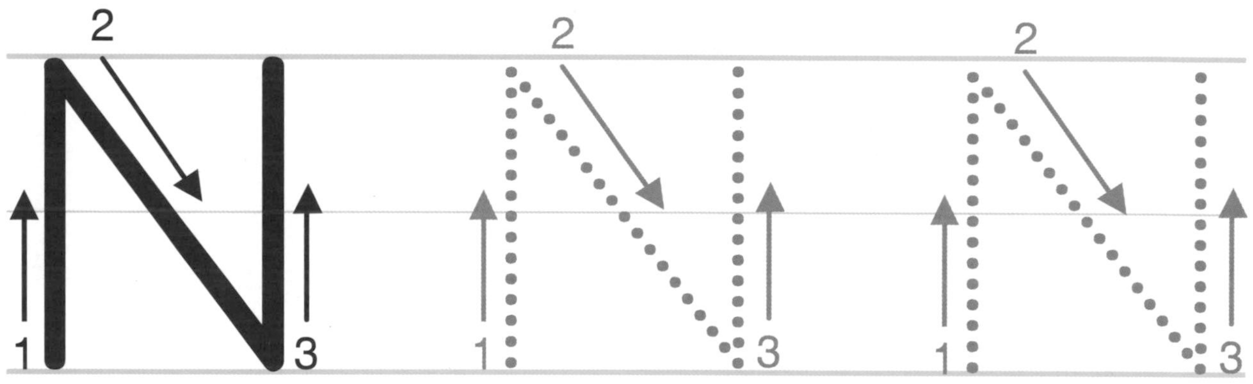

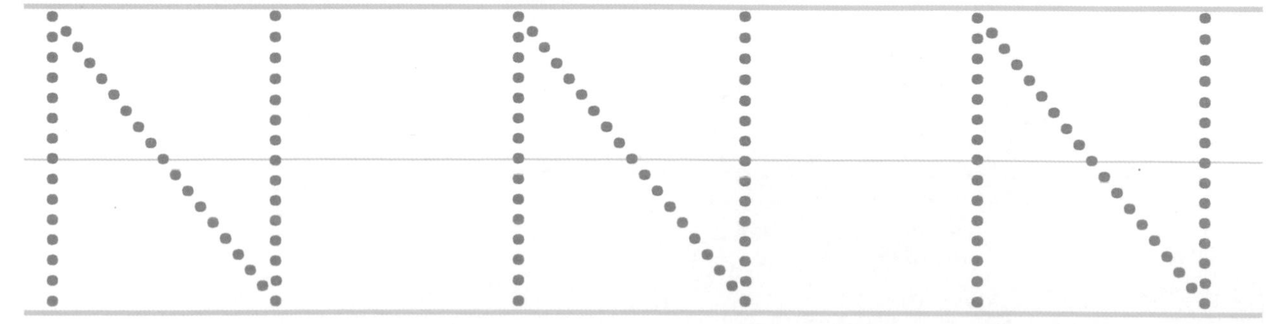

Write on your own.

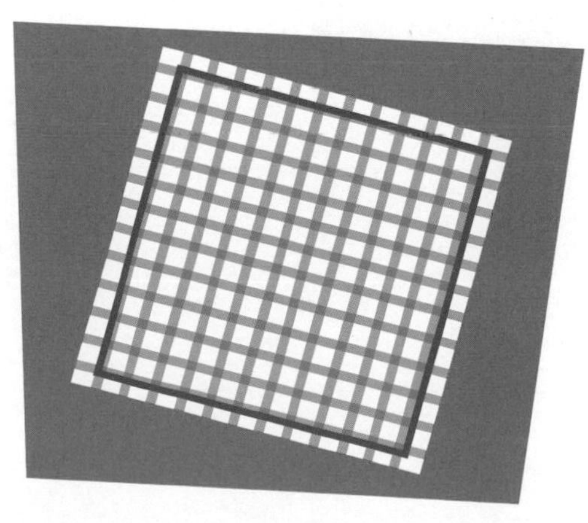

NAPKIN

NANNY

Writing

ZOO

Trace.

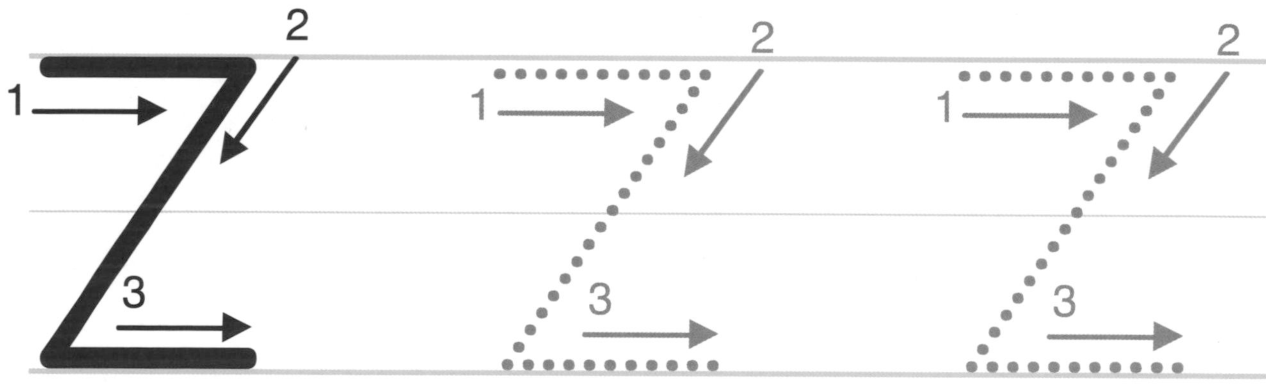

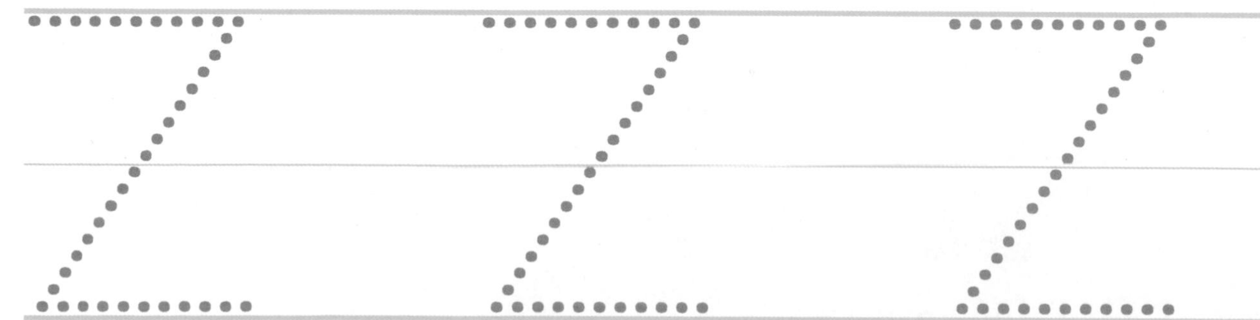

Write on your own.

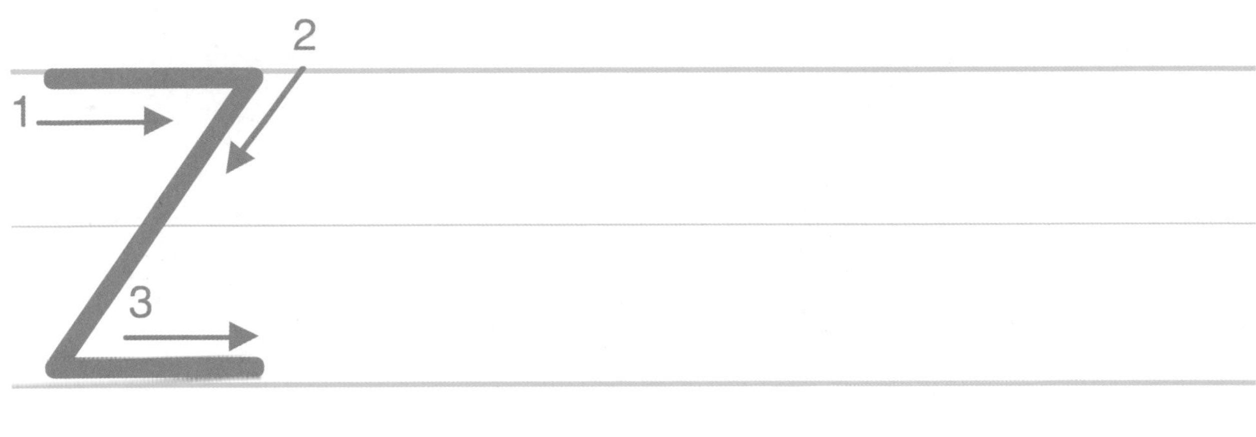

ZERO

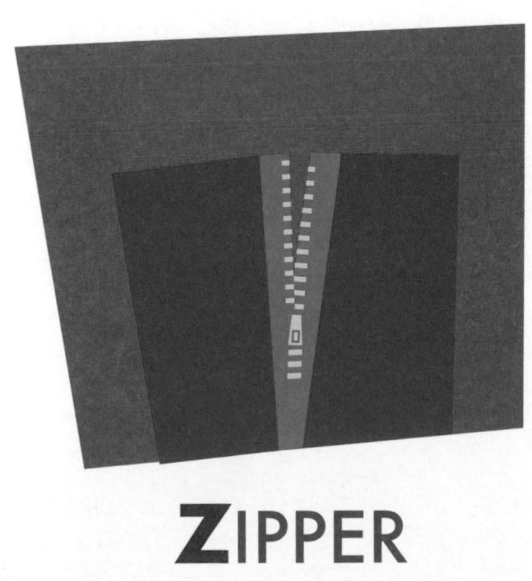

ZIPPER

Writing

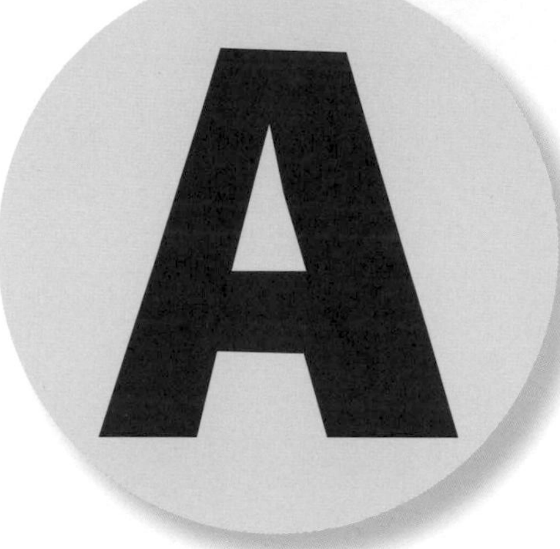

ANT

Trace.

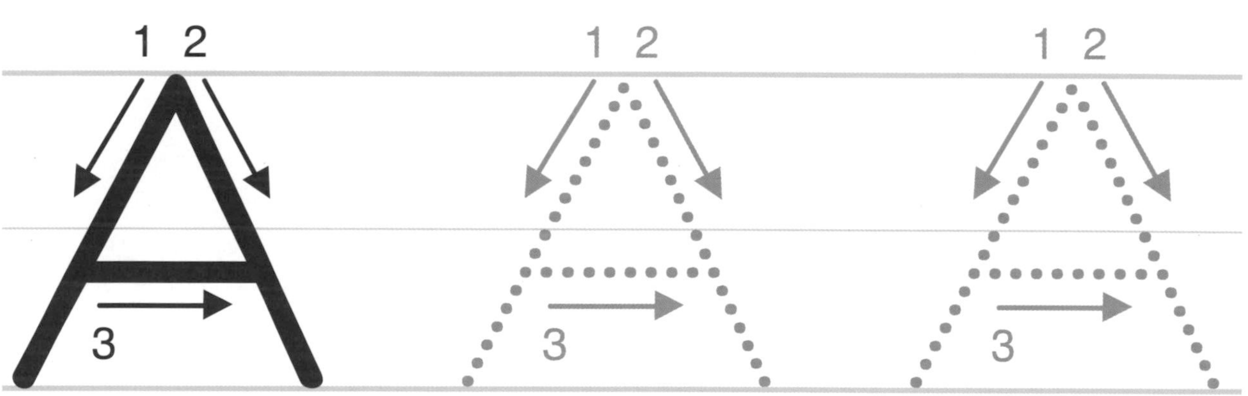

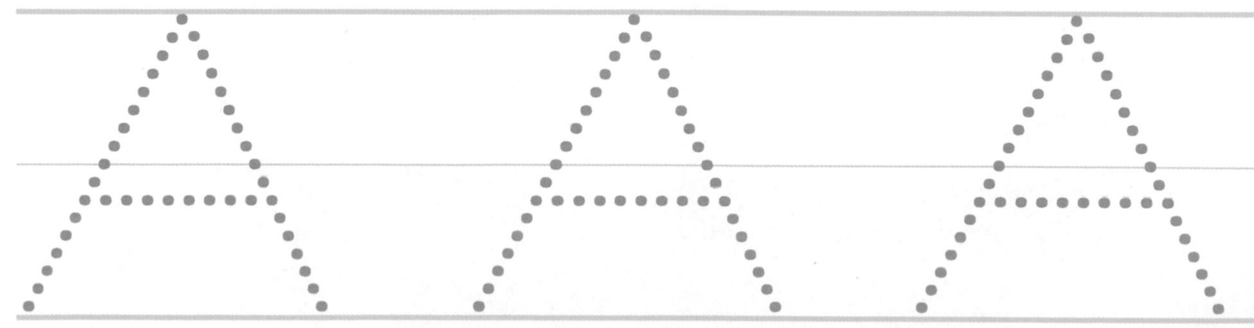

Write on your own.

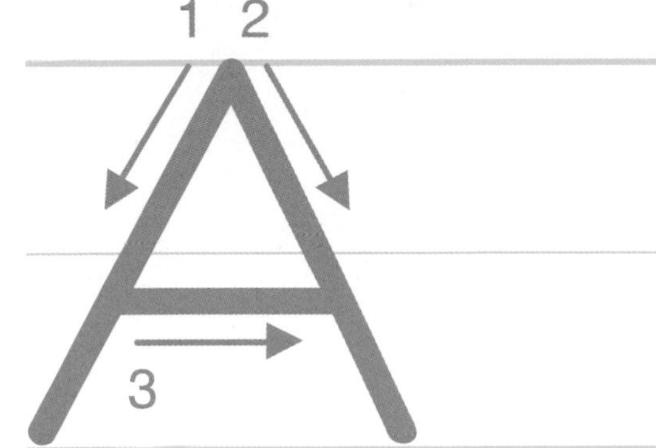

ARM

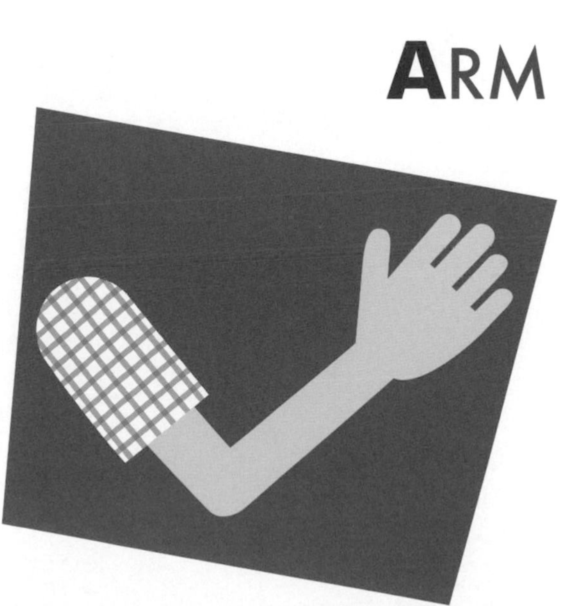

ALLIGATOR

A
B
C
D
E
F
G
H
I
J
K
L
M
N
O
P
Q
R
S
T
U
V
W
X
Y
Z

Writing

KITTEN

Trace.

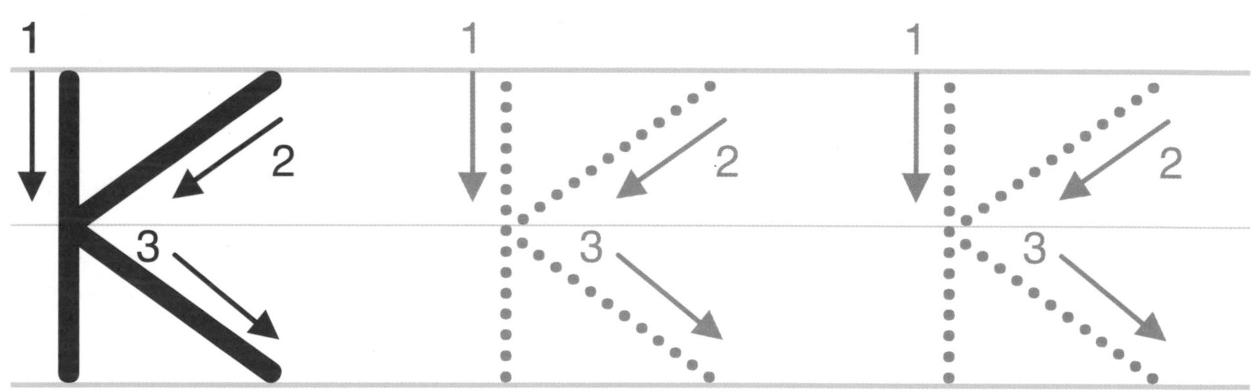

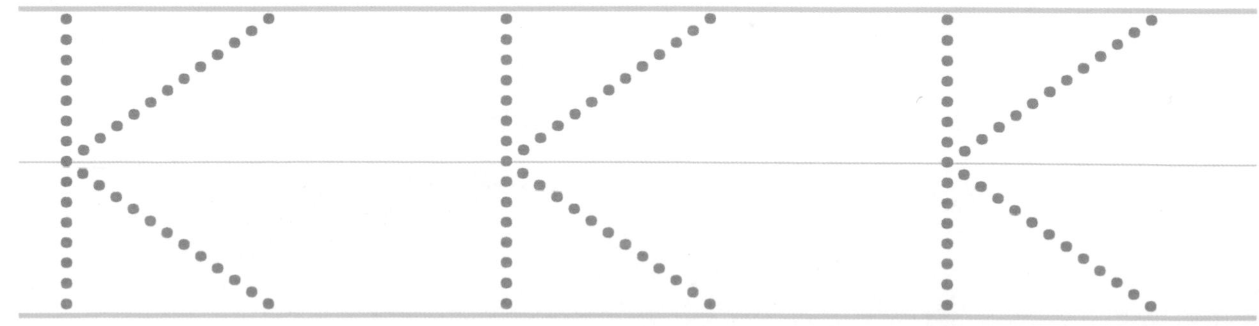

Write on your own.

KING

KITCHEN

Writing

MONSTER

Trace.

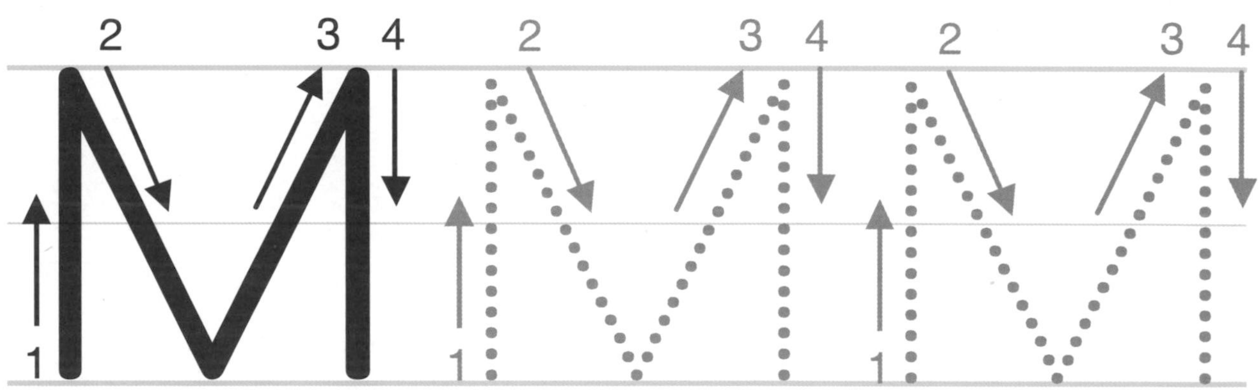

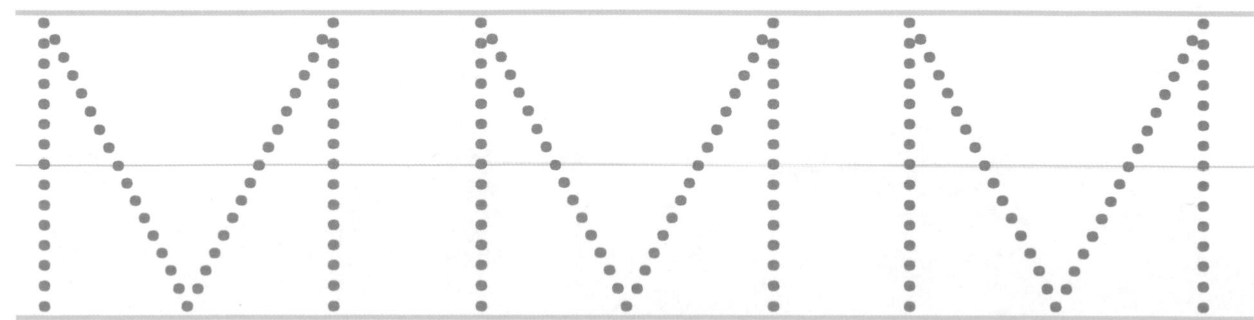

Write on your own.

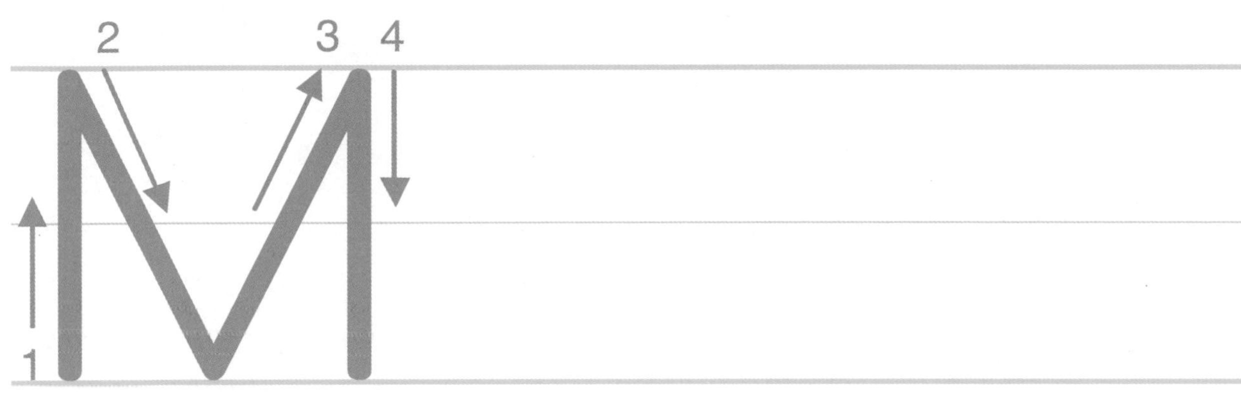

MILK

MUG

Writing

WOMAN

Trace.

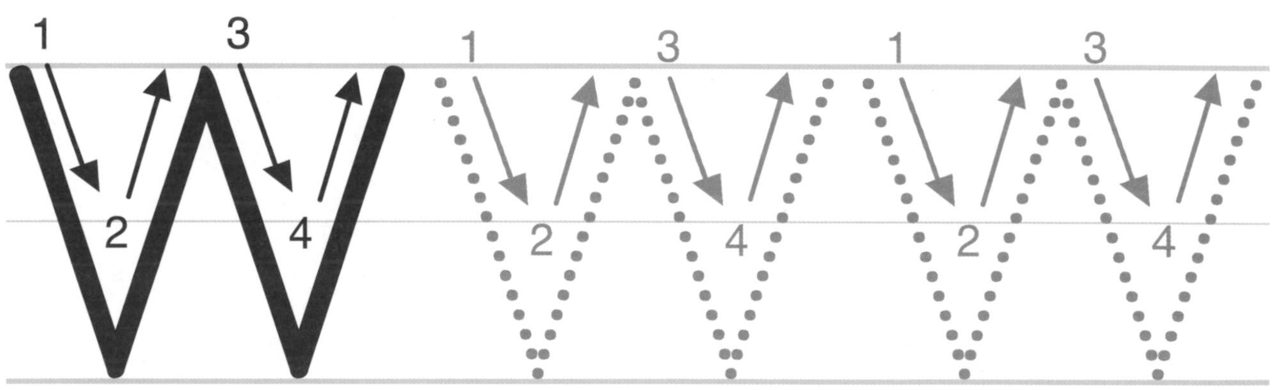

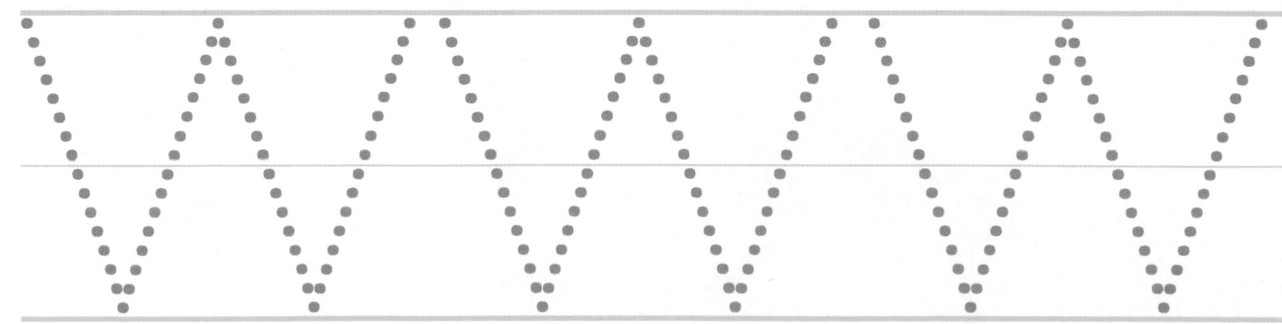

Write on your own.

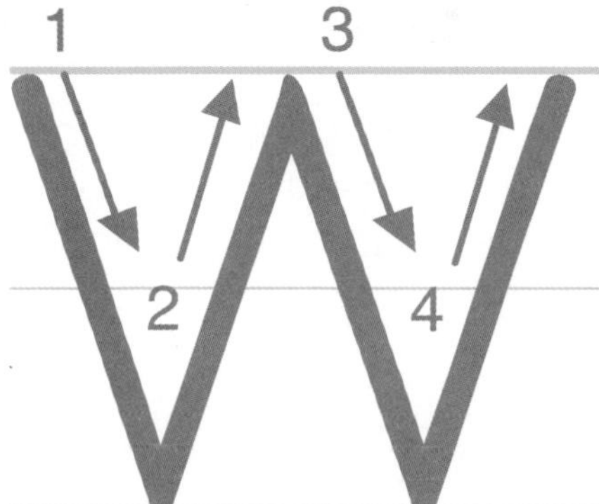

WHITE

WATER

A
B
C
D
E
F
G
H
I
J
K
L
M
N
O
P
Q
R
S
T
U
V
W
X
Y
Z

Writing

DAD

Trace.

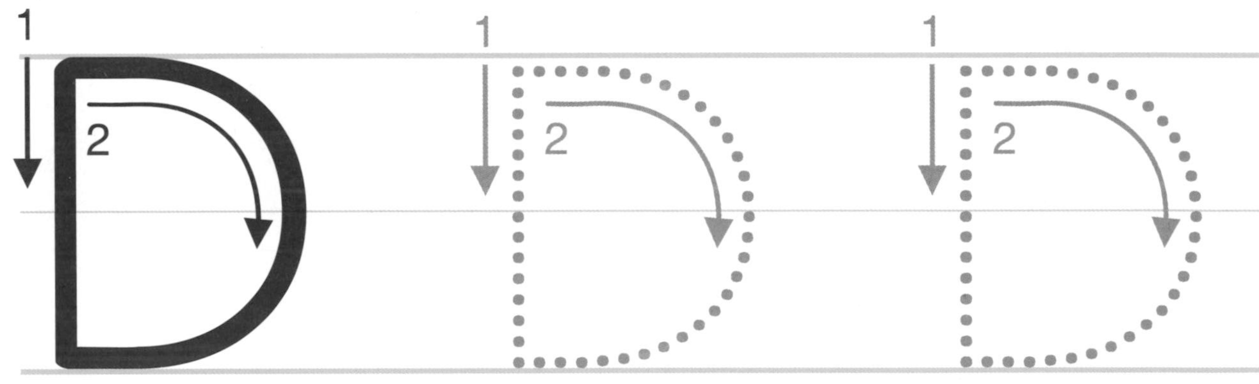

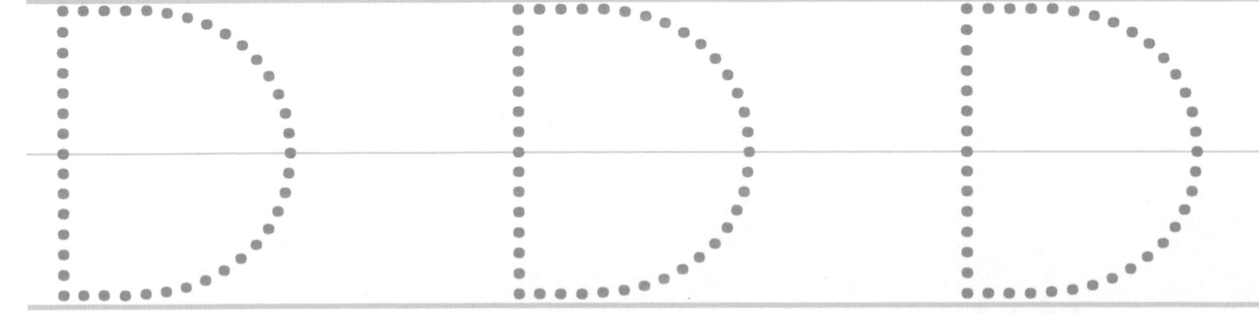

Write on your own.

A
B
C
D
E
F
G
H
I
J
K
L
M
N
O
P
Q
R
S
T
U
V
W
X
Y
Z

Writing

PUPPY

Trace.

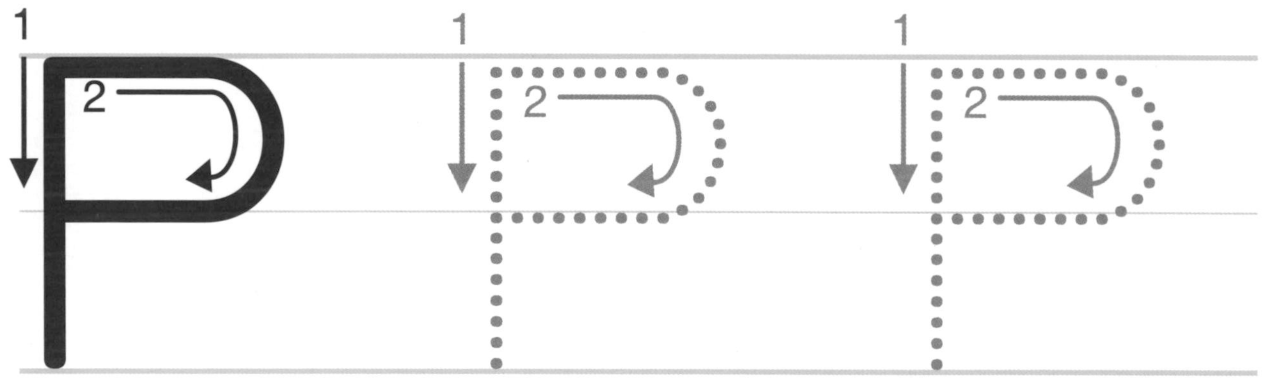

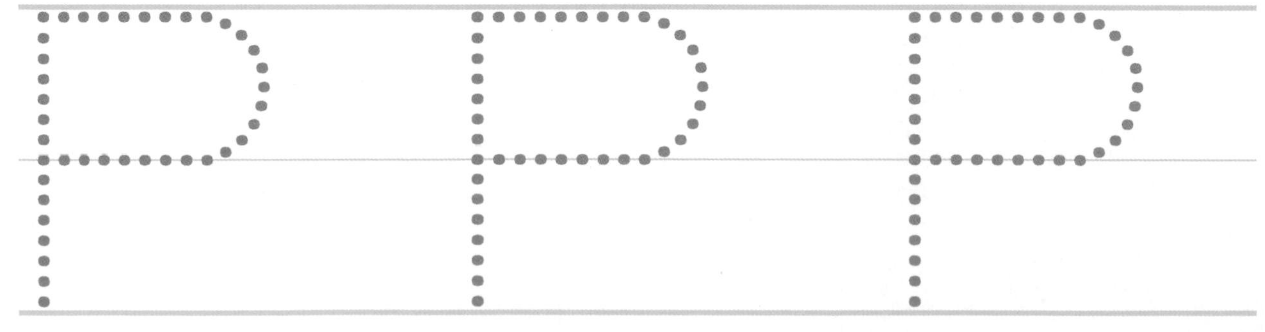

Write on your own.

PIZZA

POCKET

Writing

BIKE

Trace.

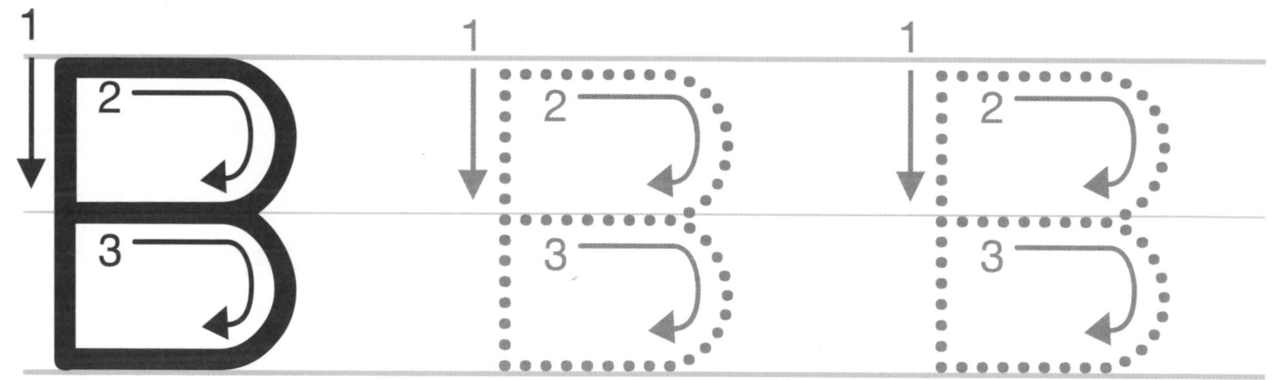

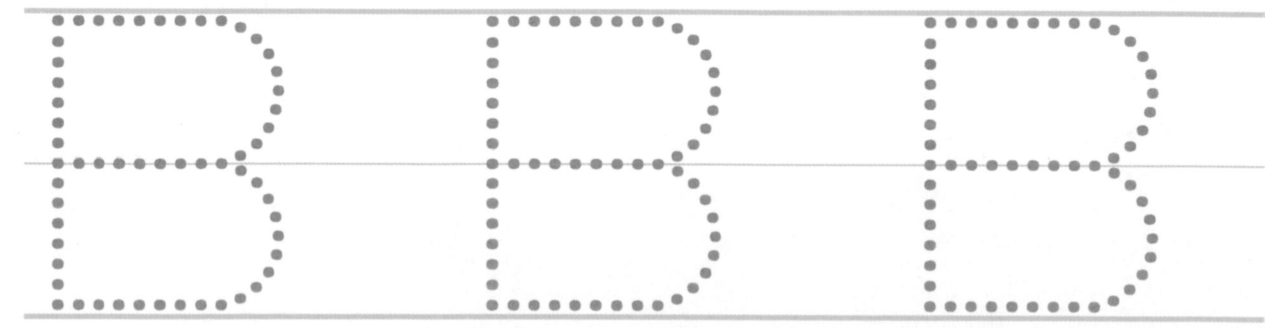

Write on your own.

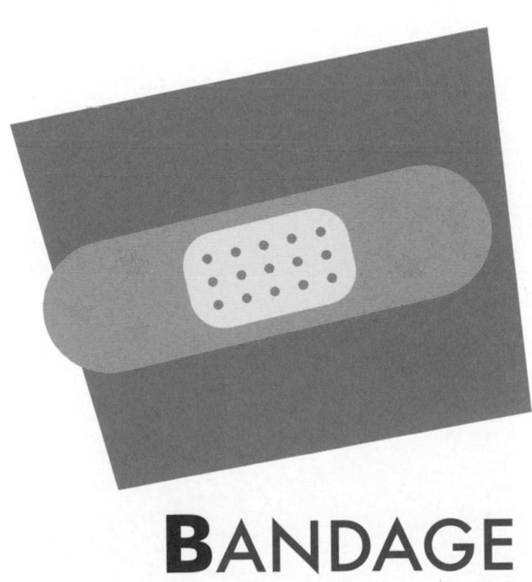

BANDAGE

BUTTER

Writing

READ

Trace.

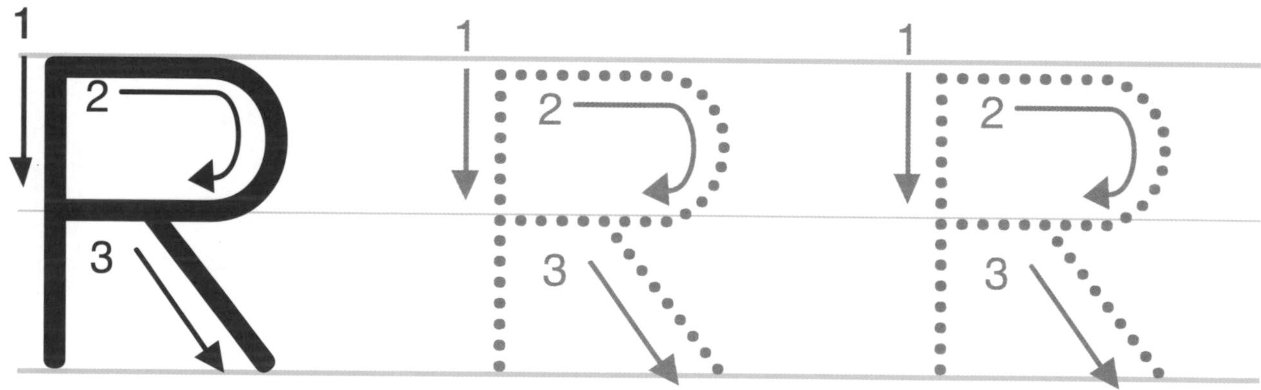

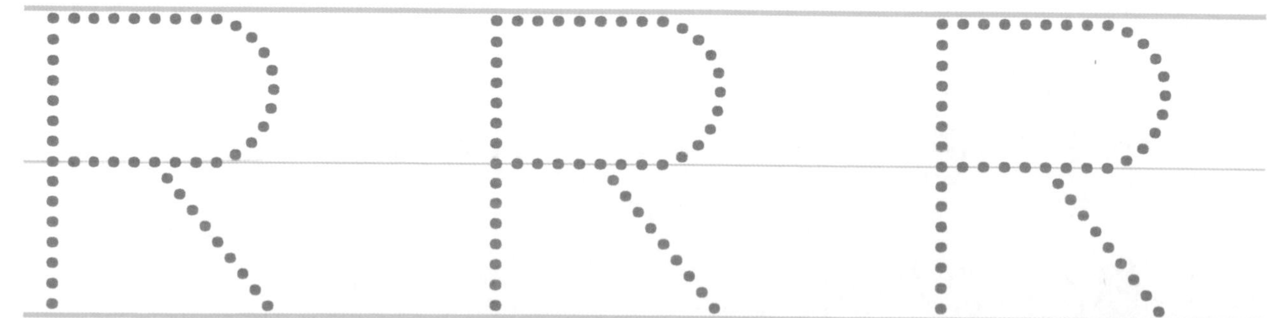

Write on your own.

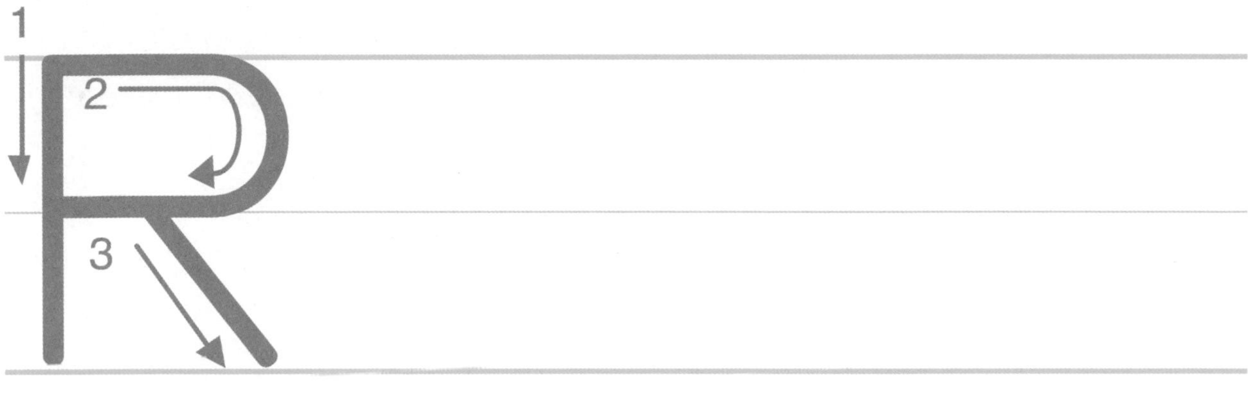

A B C D E F G H I **J** K L M N O P Q R S T U V W X Y Z

Writing

JEEP

Trace.

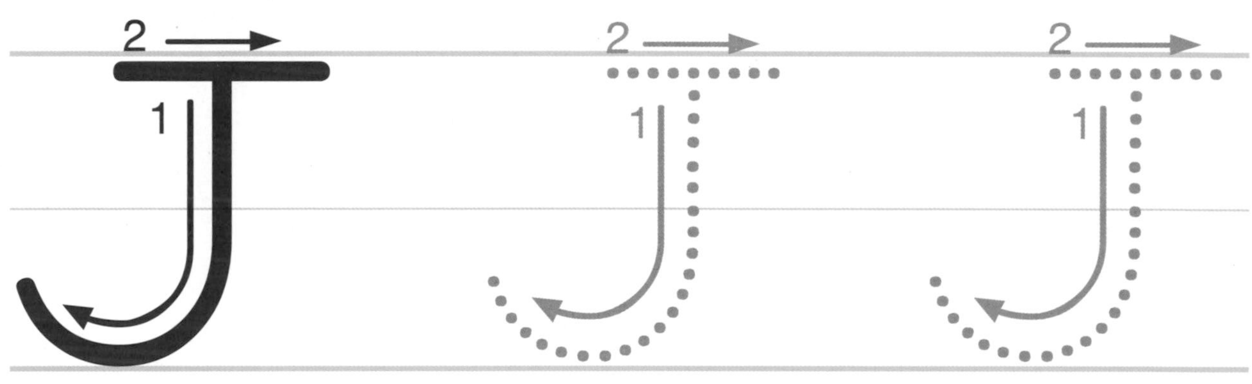

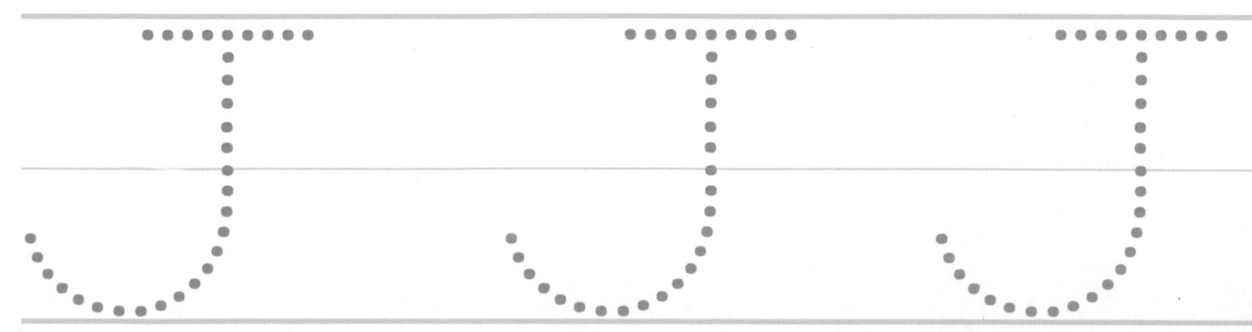

Write on your own.

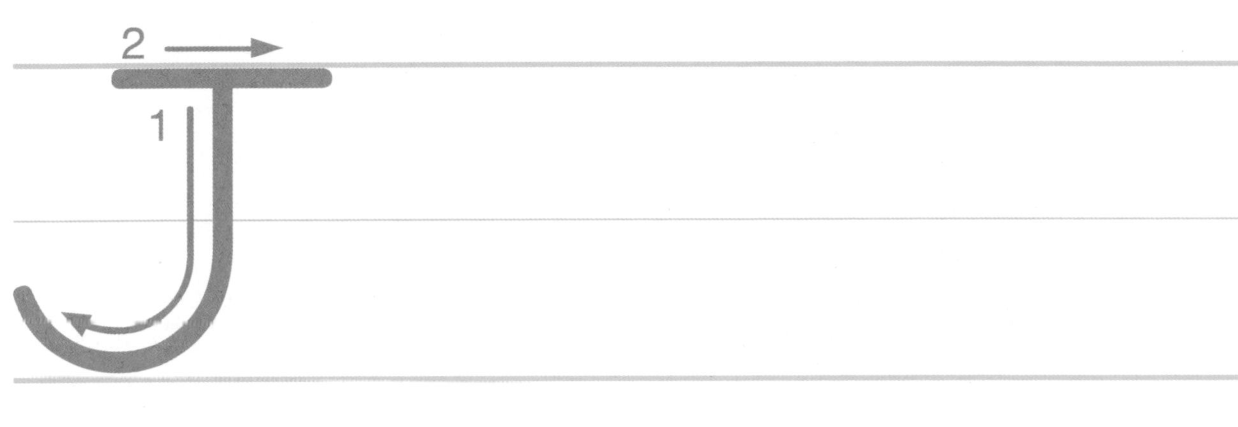

JUMP

JACKET

A
B
C
D
E
F
G
H
I
J
K
L
M
N
O
P
Q
R
S
T
U
V
W
X
Y
Z

Writing

UMBRELLA

Trace.

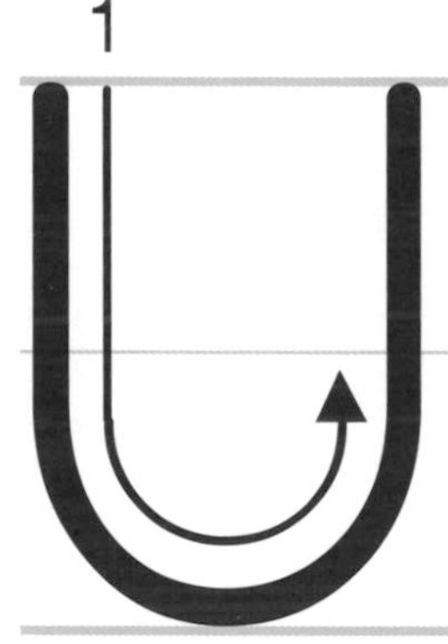

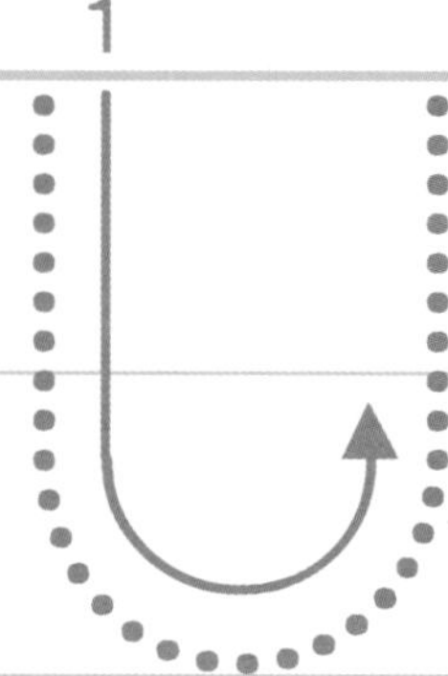

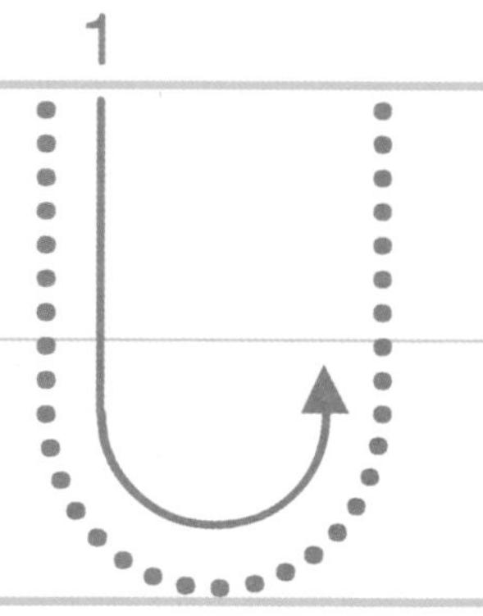

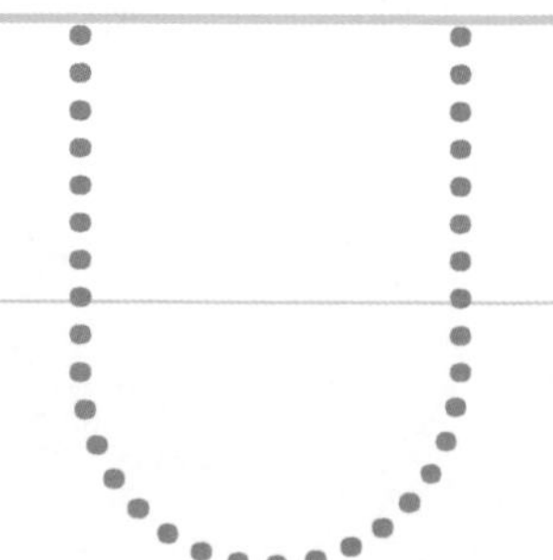

Write on your own.

UPSIDE-DOWN

UNDERWEAR

Writing

CANDY

Trace.

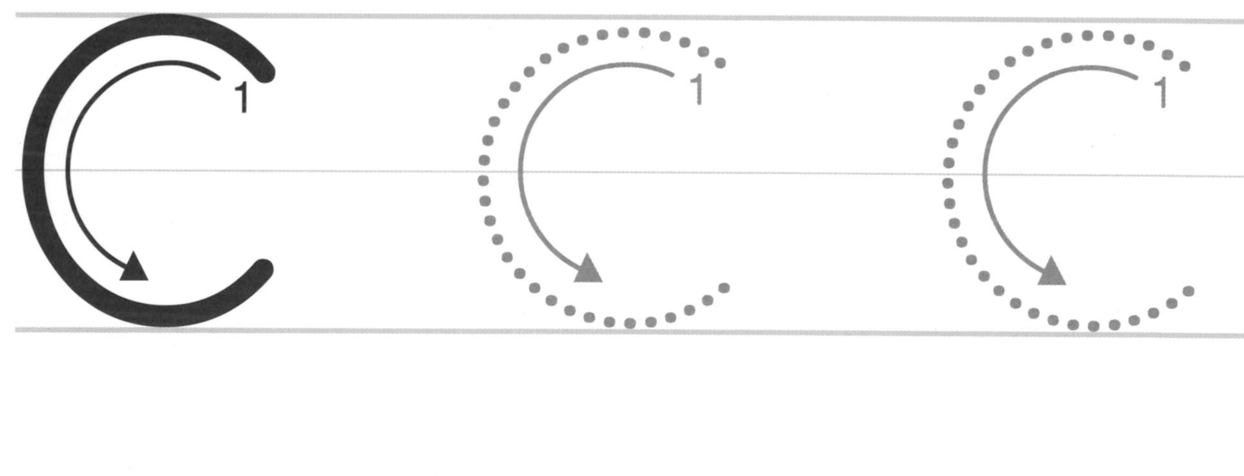

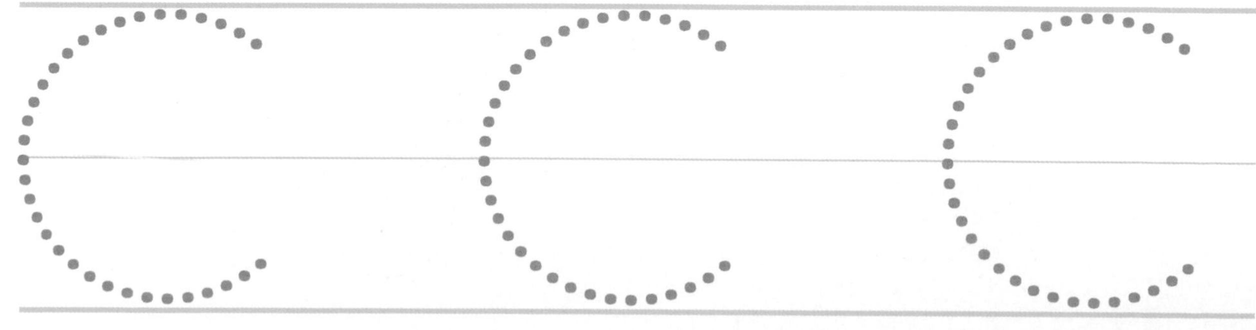

Write on your own.

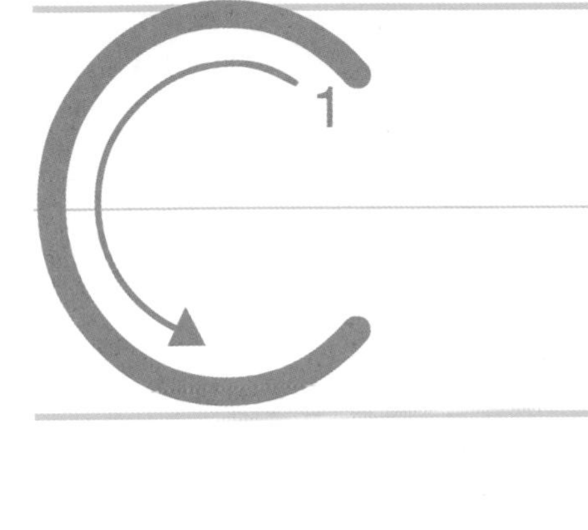

CREAM

CAT

Writing

GIRL

Trace.

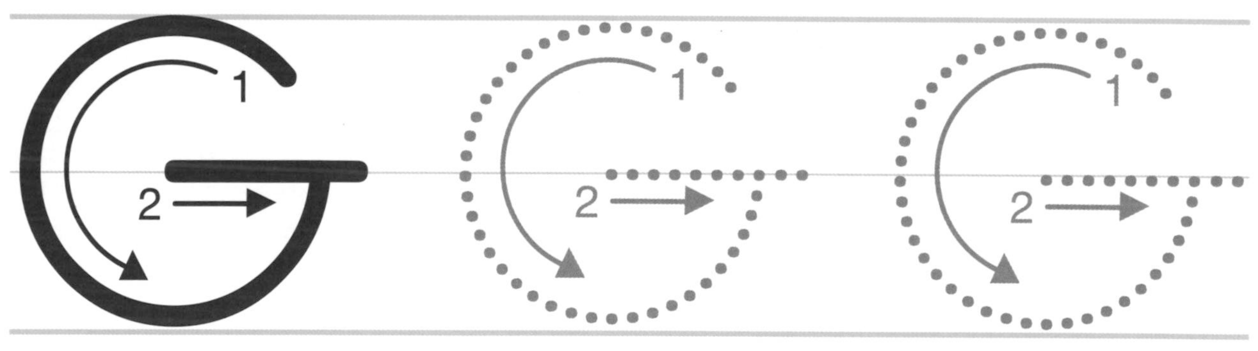

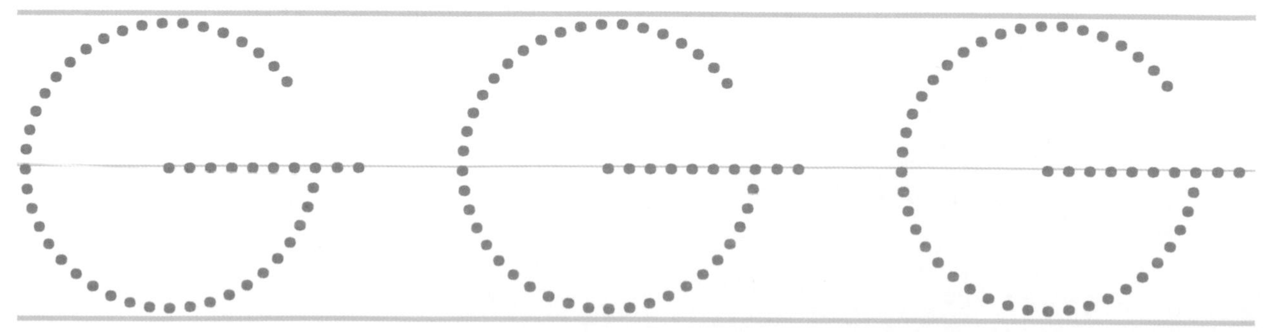

Write on your own.

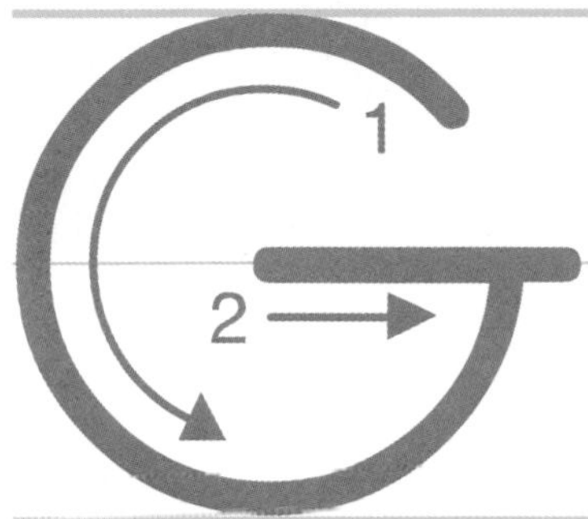

GREEN

GLOVES

Writing

SNOW

Trace.

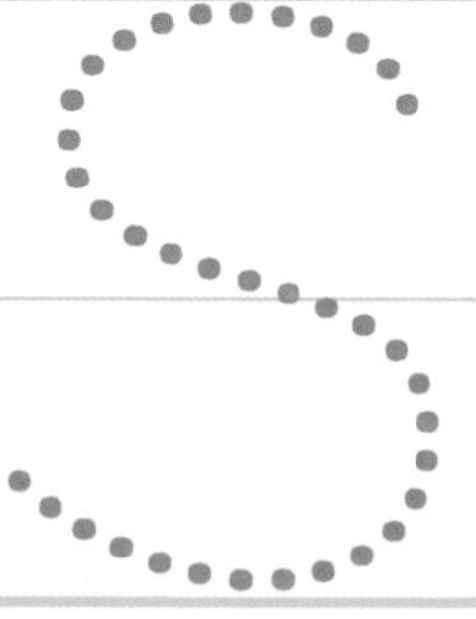

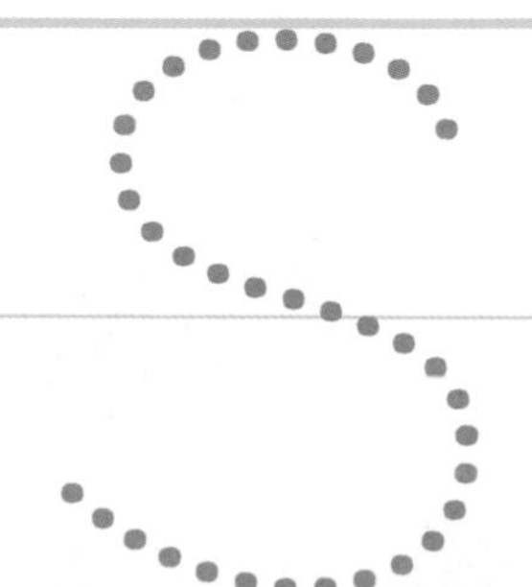

Write on your own.

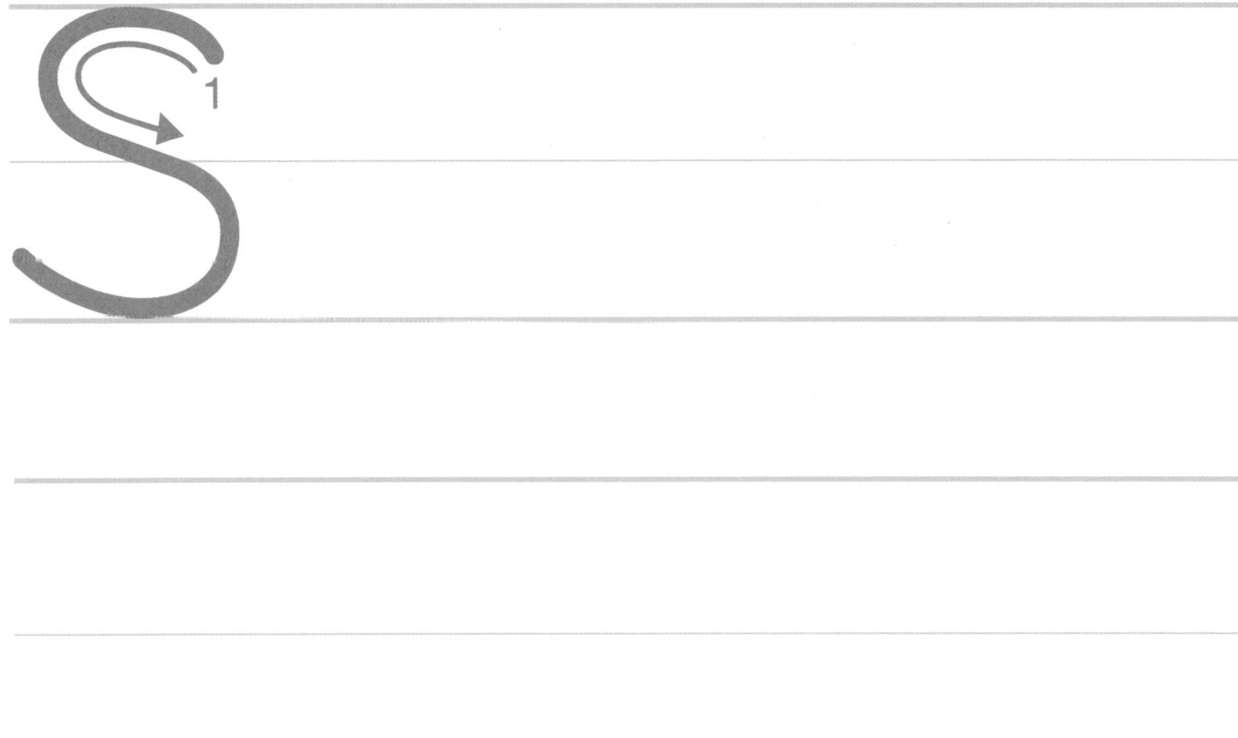

STOP

SCARF

A
B
C
D
E
F
G
H
I
J
K
L
M
N
O
P
Q
R
S
T
U
V
W
X
Y
Z

Writing

ORANGE

Trace.

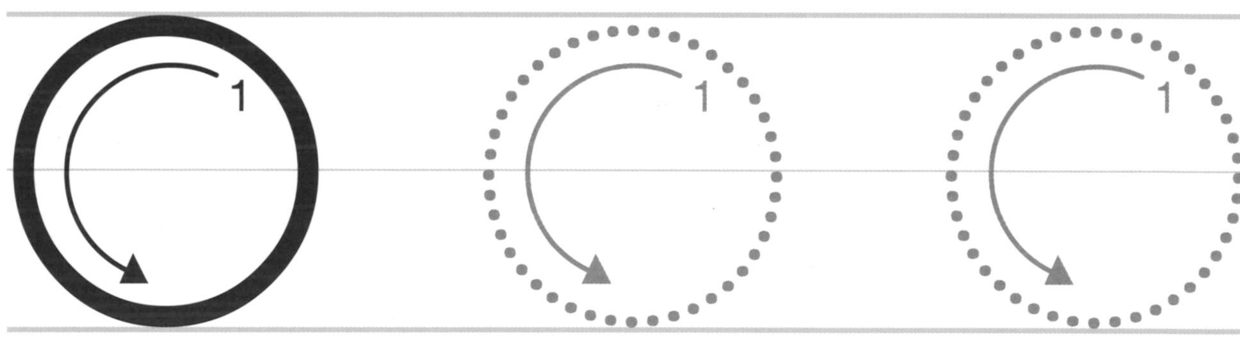

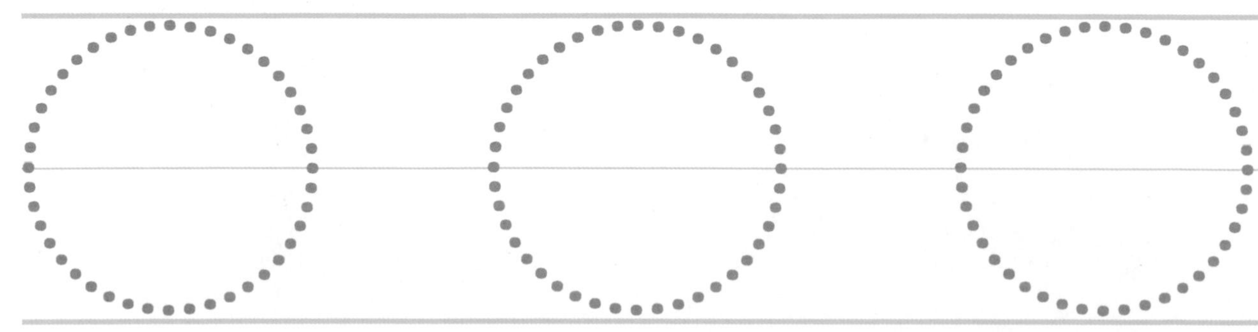

Write on your own.

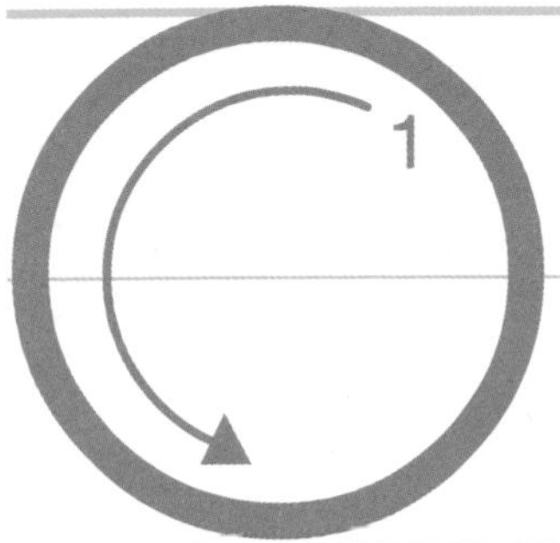

ONION

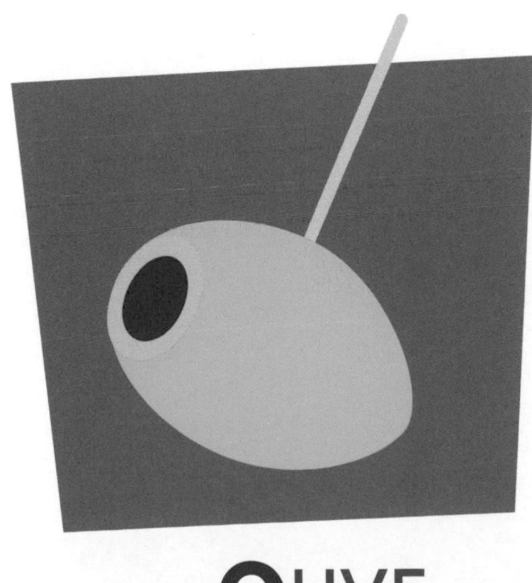

OLIVE

Writing

QUEEN

Trace.

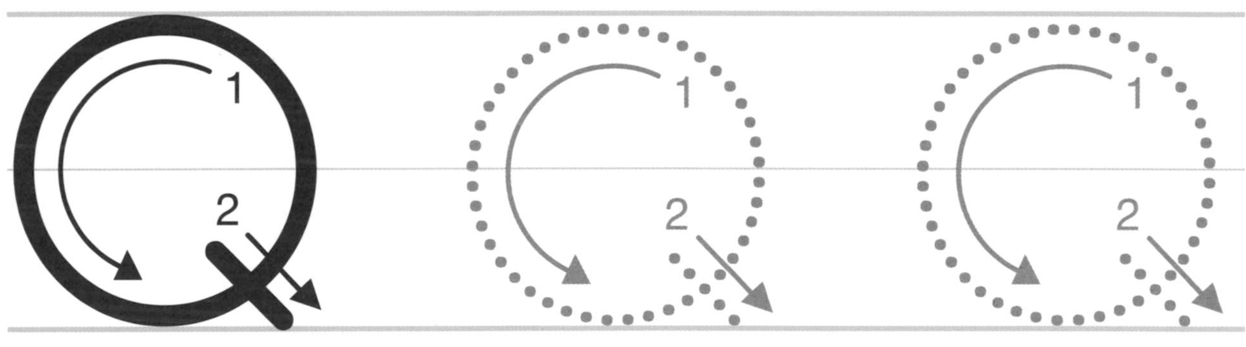

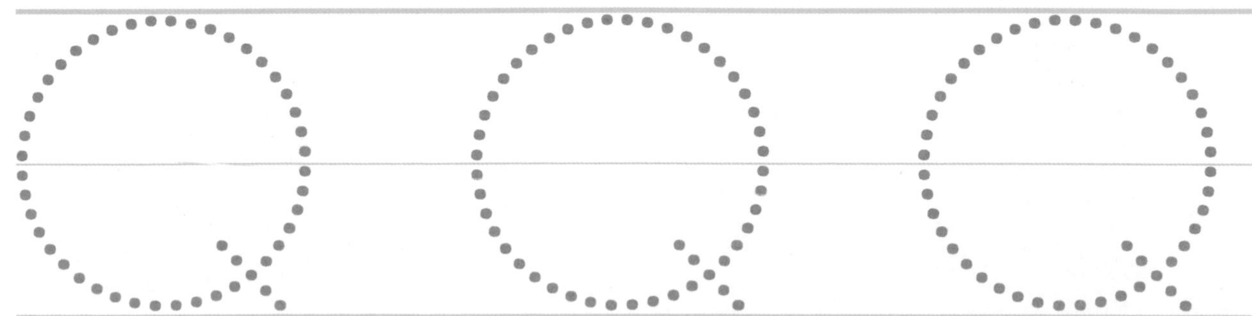

Write on your own.

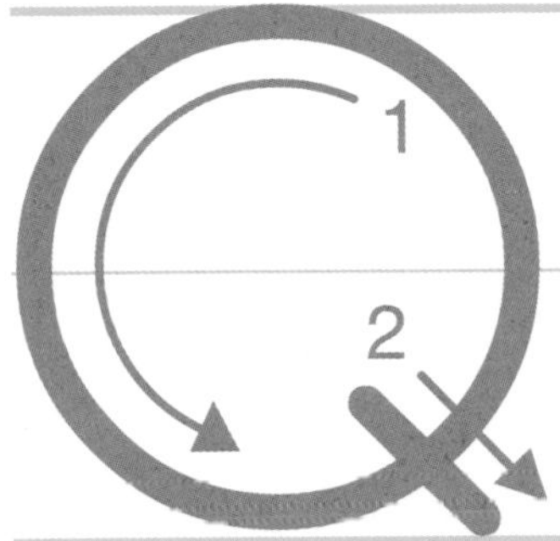

QUARTER

QUACK

A
B
C
D
E
F
G
H
I
J
K
L
M
N
O
P
Q
R
S
T
U
V
W
X
Y
Z

REVIEW

Letters

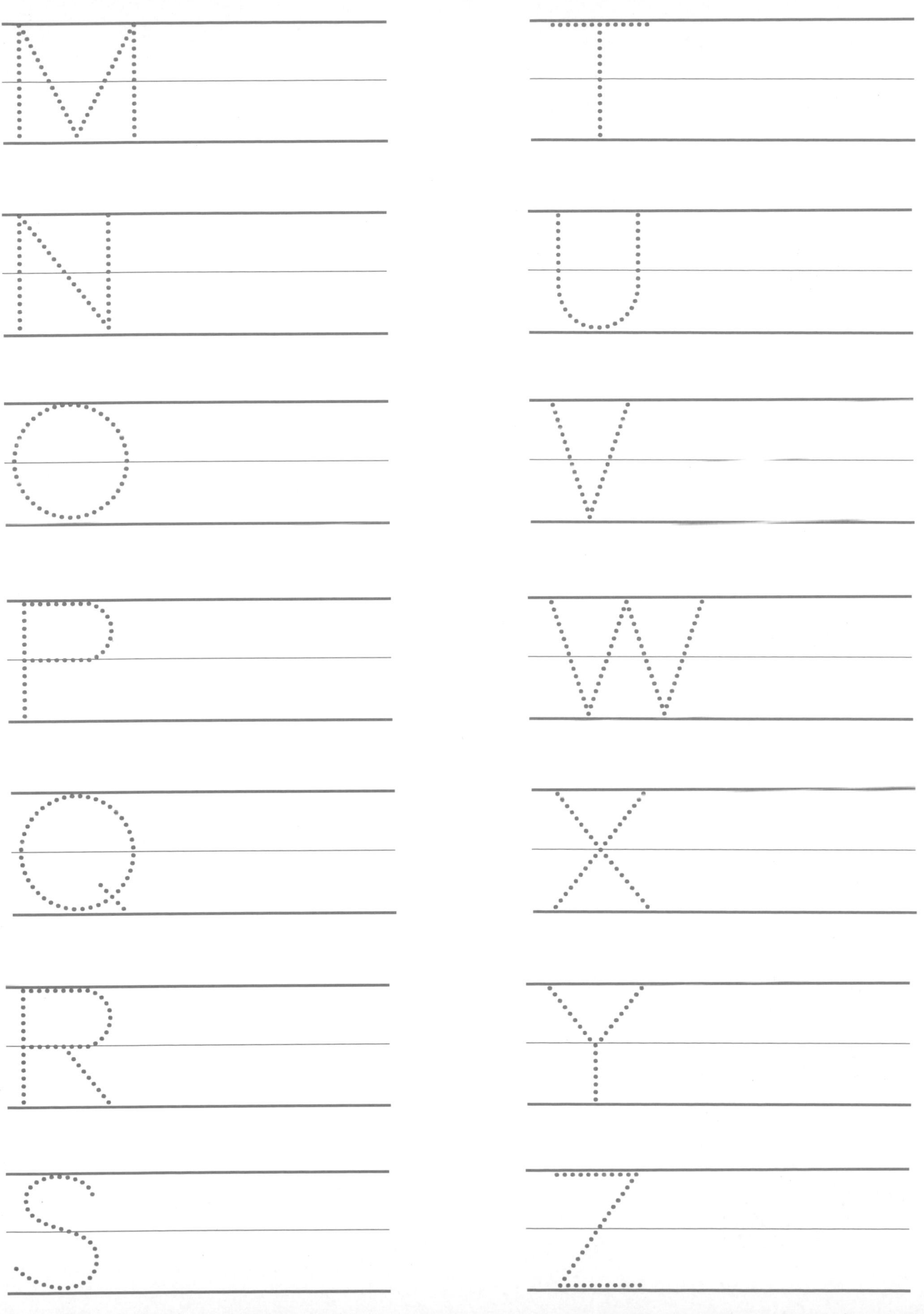

M
N
O
P
Q
R
S
T
U
V
W
X
Y
Z

Writing

Trace.

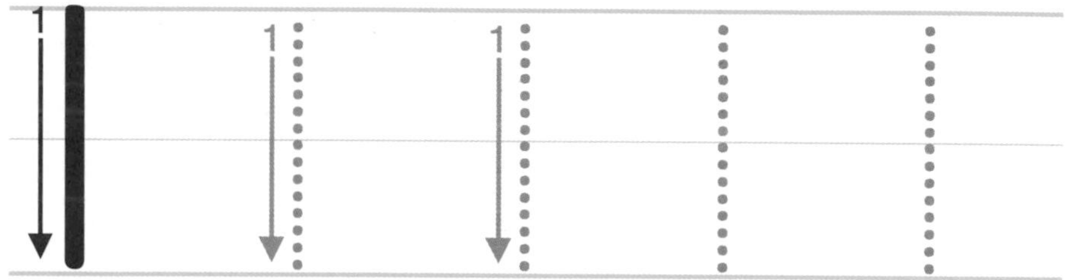

Write on your own.

Trace.

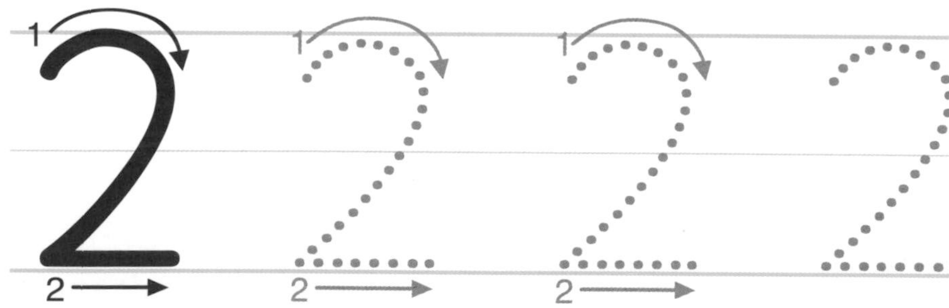

Write on your own.

1
2
3
4
5
6
7
8
9
10

3

Trace.

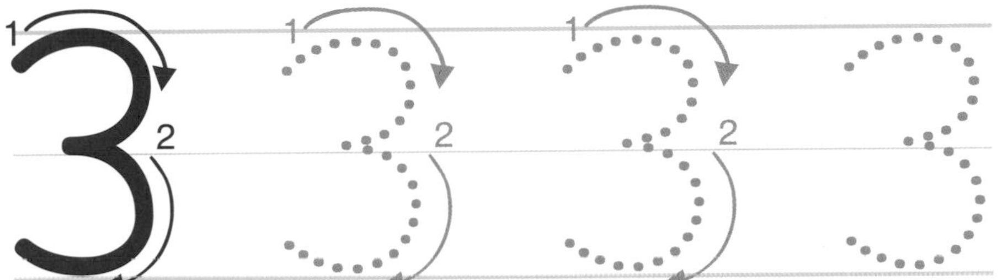

Write on your own.

4

Trace.

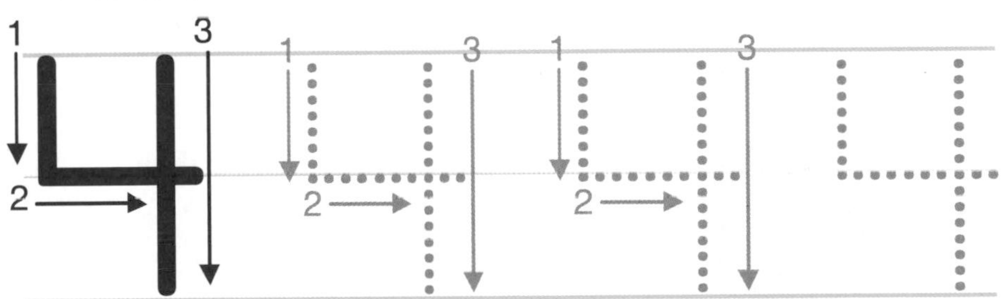

Write on your own.

Writing

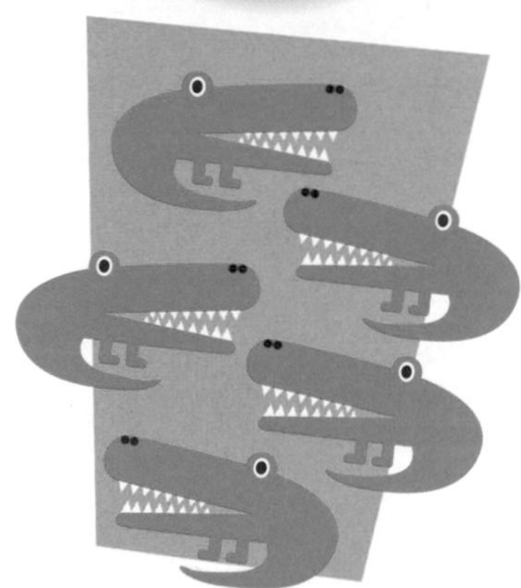

Trace.

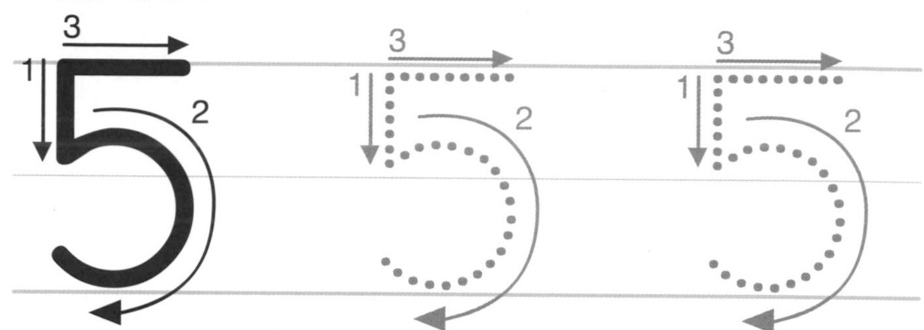

Write on your own.

Trace.

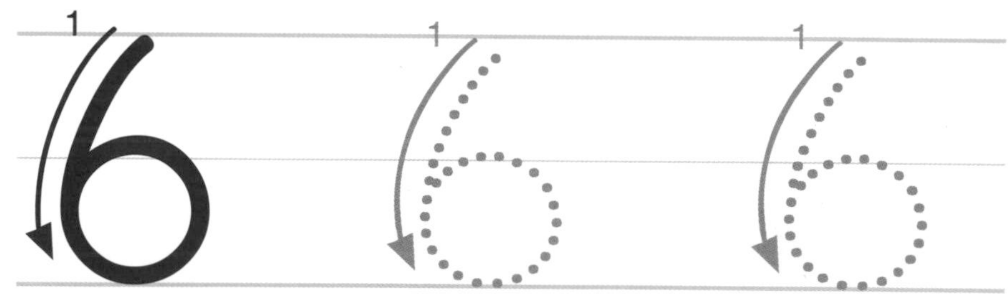

Write on your own.

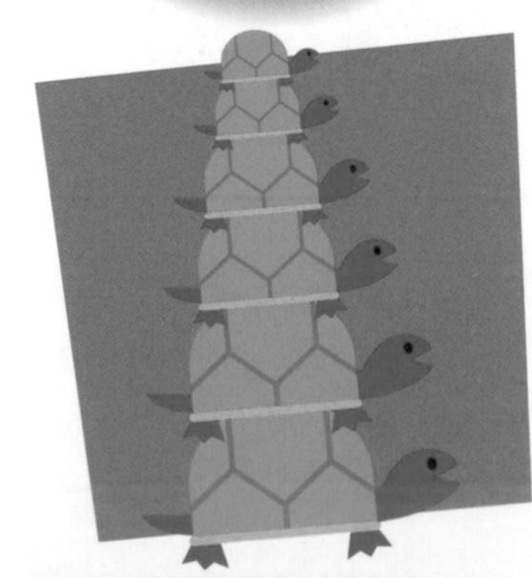

Trace.

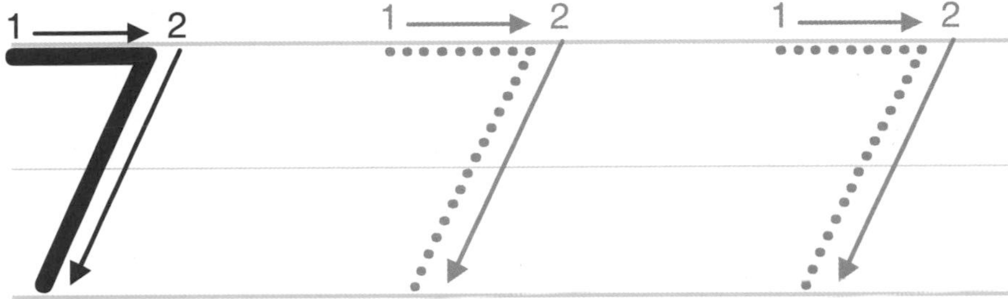

Write on your own.

Trace.

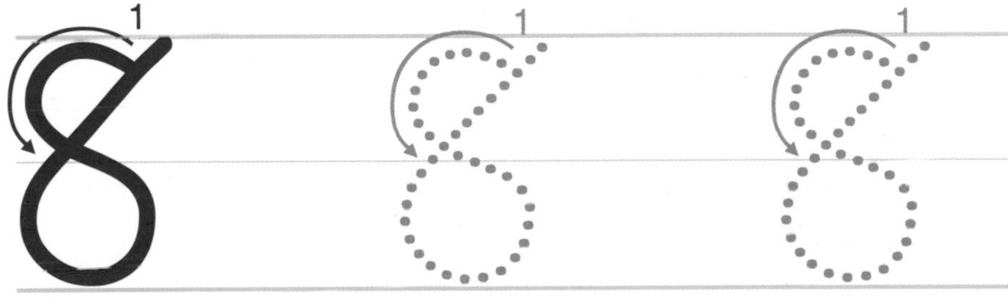

Write on your own.

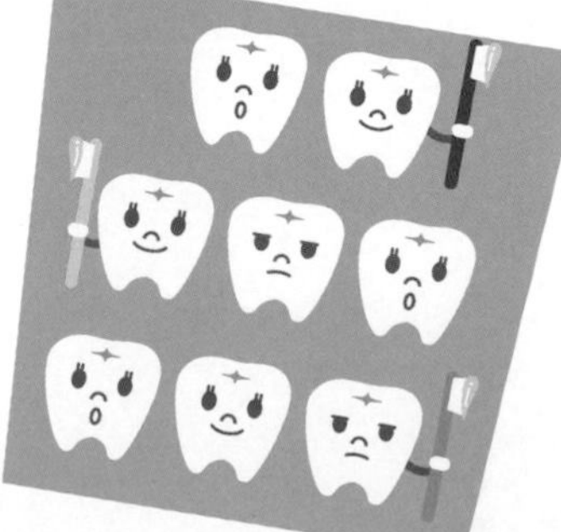

Writing

Trace.

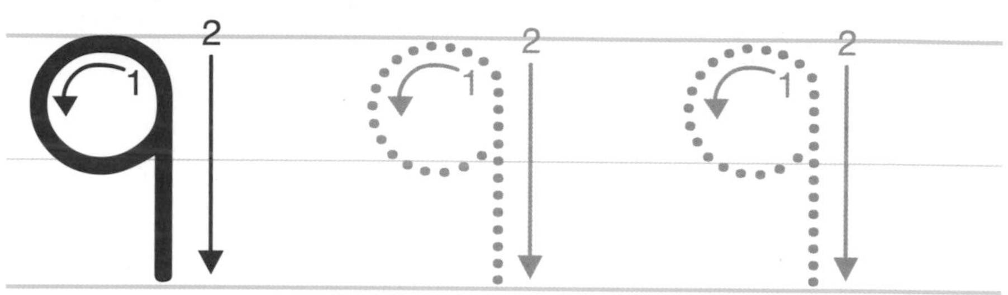

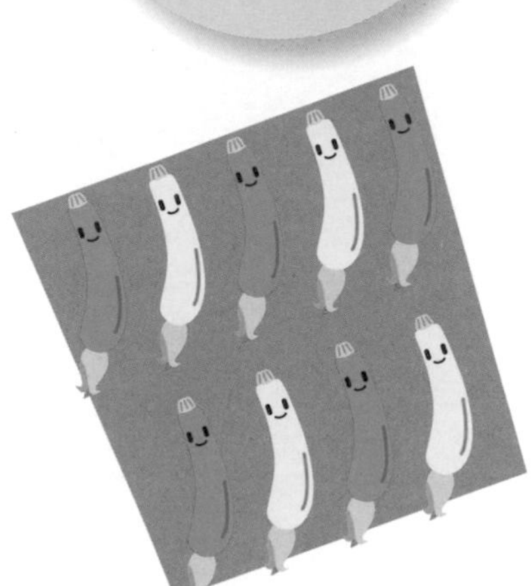

Write on your own.

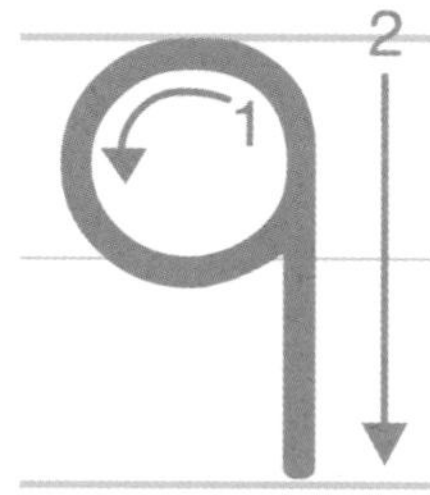

Trace.

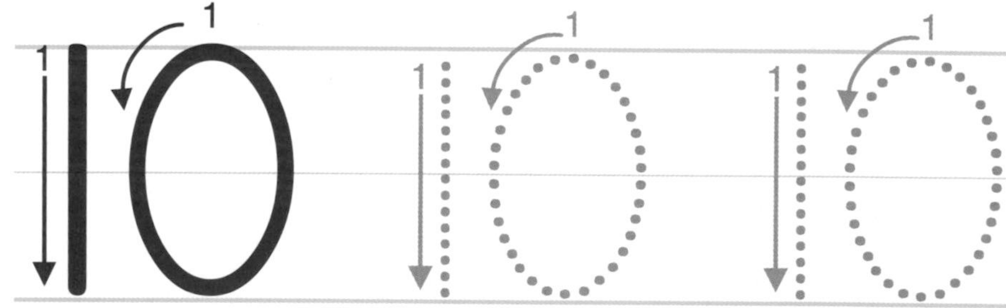

Write on your own.

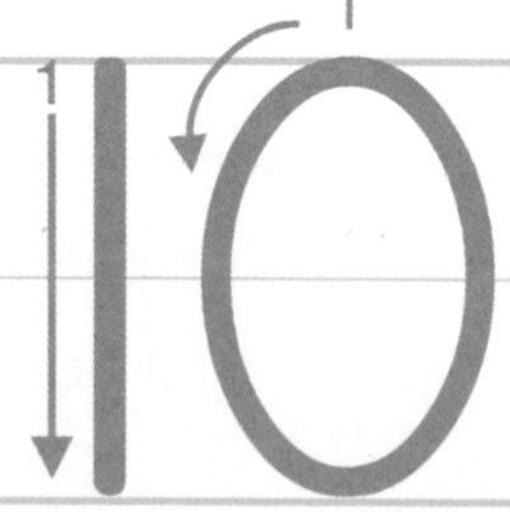

REVIEW

Numbers

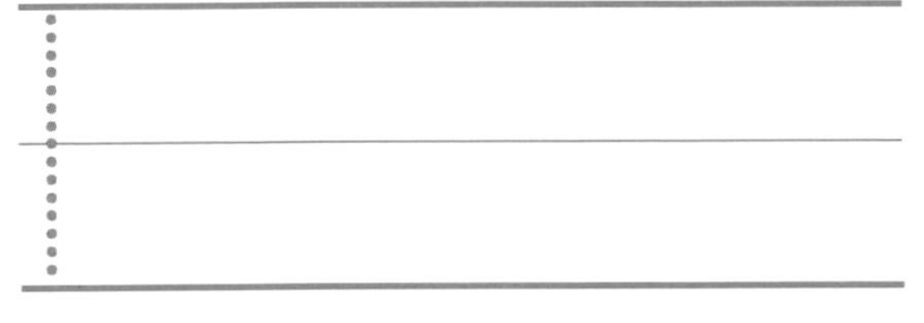

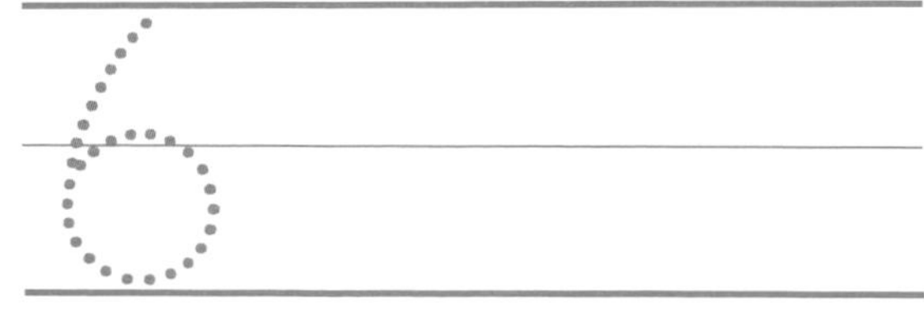

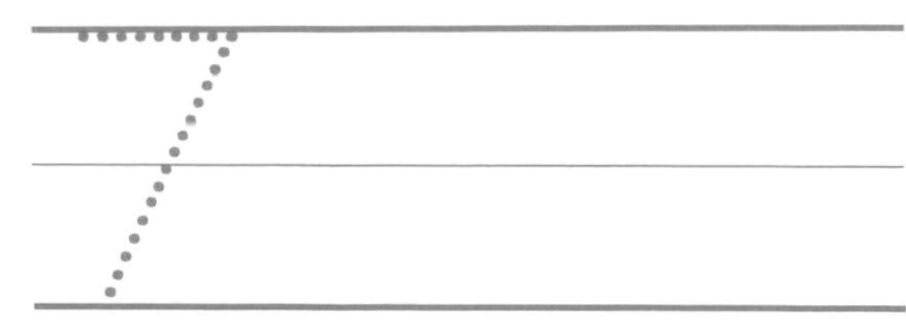

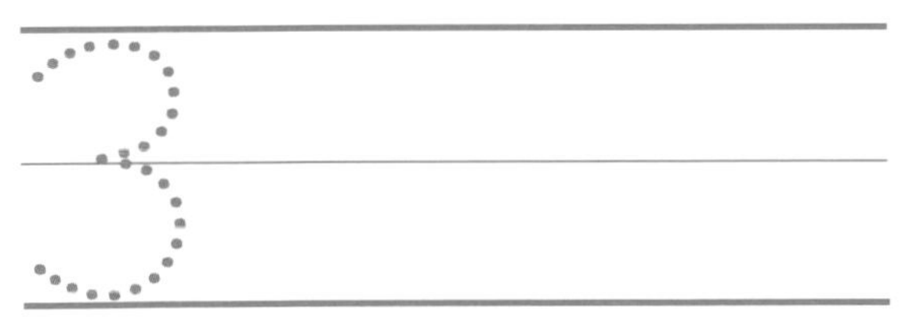

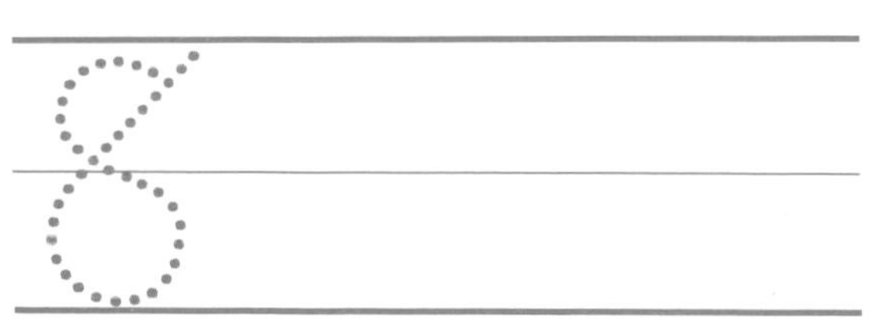

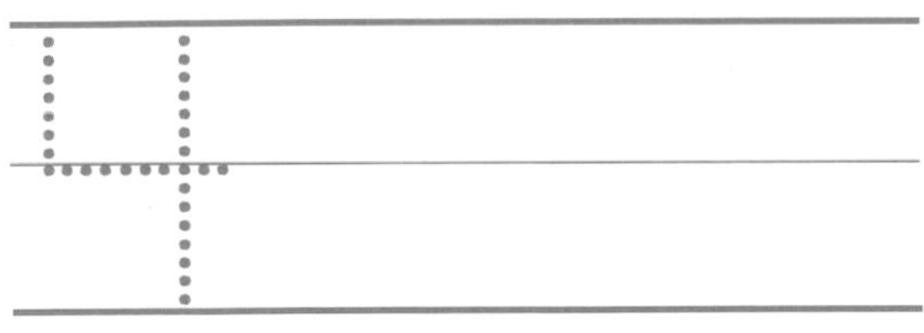

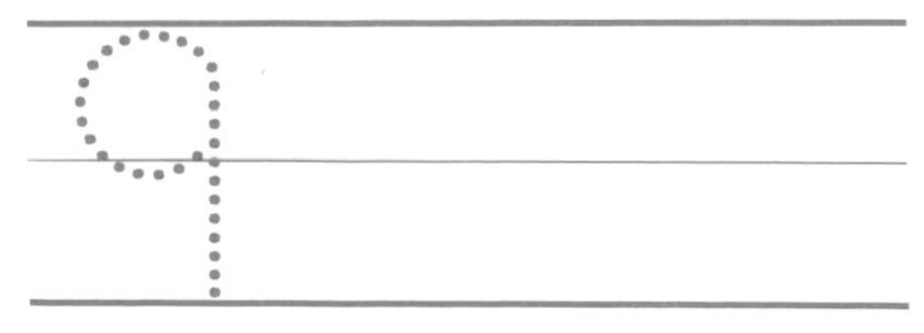

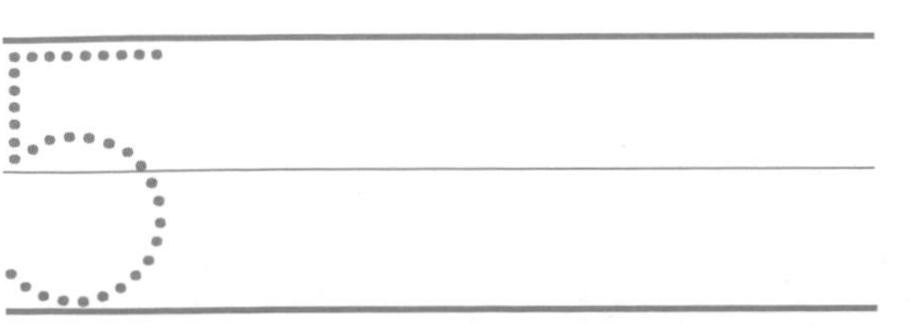

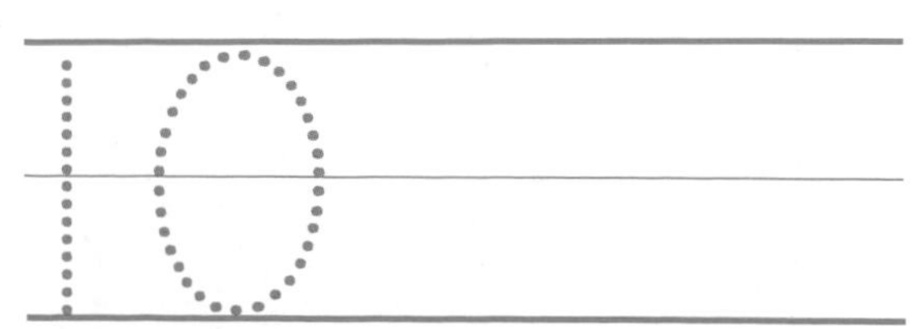

1 2 3 4 5 6 7 8 9 10

date

first name

last name

★ ★ ★ ★ I Can WRITE ★ ★ ★ ★

Uppercase Letters and Numbers 1–10